To Sara
Who walks a
similar path and hears
similar thoughts as we
listen.

♡ Sandy

DEVELOP YOUR INNER LEADERSHIP
FOR BETTER HEALTH AND SUCCESS.

ATTUNEMENT:
SIX PRACTICES TO CONNECT
TO THE POWERFUL LEADER INSIDE

If Not You, Then Who?

SANDY SCHULTZ

BALBOA.PRESS
A DIVISION OF HAY HOUSE

Balboa Press books may be ordered through booksellers or by contacting:

Balboa Press
A Division of Hay House
1663 Liberty Drive
Bloomington, IN 47403
www.balboapress.com
844-682-1282

Print information available on the last page.

ISBN: 979-8-7652-3939-1 (sc)
ISBN: 979-8-7652-3941-4 (hc)
ISBN: 979-8-7652-3940-7 (e)

Library of Congress Control Number: 2023903376

Balboa Press rev. date: 03/17/2023

What Is the Six Minutes Daily Practice?

The Six Minutes Daily practice starts with three minutes or so of breathing slowly, allowing the light of the day to flow through the crown of your head and down through all your body's pathways, allowing the fire from deep in the earth to flow up through your feet, and feeling both the light and the fire swirl around and energize your heart and core. Just breathe in the *presence* of the moment.

Then, for two minutes or so, breathe in your *intentions* for the day—a word, value, or phrase to ground you. Perhaps it is just the intention to feel inspiration. Ideally, write them down in a journal.

And then for about a minute, breathe in *gratitude* for something or someone you appreciate or have learned from. And perhaps even picture your breath as a golden thread of thanks from your heart to theirs. Again, ideally write them down in a journal.

For my family from whom I have learned what's most important

Chris, Phil, Jack, Jimmy, Nikki, Brolin, Miguel, Tom
And my dear mom, Irene

Contents

Acknowledgments...xi

Preface... xiii

1   Beginnings...1

2   Reflections 5

3   Key Reflection Questions for Journaling.....................................10

4   The Six Practices of Attunement for Authentic,
     Deepened Leadership 18

     a.   Awareness...19

     b.   Acceptance... 24

     c.   Articulation 28

     d.   Alignment..37

     e.   Appreciation...41

     f.   Action..42

5   The Practice 44

6   Quiet Shift; Seismic Change 166

References and Inspiring Books I've Read on This Journey........... 167

About the Author.. 169

Acknowledgments

All we do in life is part of a process and cycle that includes many people and experiences. This book is a profound example of that cycle. I may have written the words, but it took a beloved village to help the ideas emerge and come to life. I am filled with much gratitude.

For all my teachers, Guy & Kay Napier, Tom Moore, Robert Holden, Donna Good, Joe McCarthy, Nick Craig, Kellan Fluckiger, Lynne McAuliffe, Bob Berky, Craig Chalquist, Ron & Mary Hulnick, and many others, I am so grateful for your mentorship.

For my family, both biological and from my heart including Sue, Tim, Donna, Kathryn, Meg, Pammie, Lydia, Sue B, Daniela, Liza, Kat, Ginny, Margi, Jane, Lisa, Paige and Wes. Thanks for always being there and for being amazing listeners and lifelines.

For all of my students and clients that teach me more every day.

And for my patient, wise editorial team, Julie Kling and Sami Thune.

And for the wisdom and energy of family and friends no longer here, especially my dad Phil, friend Beth Bash, and stepfather, Milt and for all the muses and angels who gave me the roadmap.

Preface

So, what is attunement? According to the *Merriam-Webster Dictionary*, the word *attune* means

- To bring into harmony
- To make responsively aware
- To recognize, understand and engage with someone's emotional state, including your own

Attunement is often referred to as a relationship "superpower." It provides the bond to deeper understanding, connections and flow in every kind of relationship.

For our purposes, *Attunement* is a book to help us reclaim the lost balance between internal and external drives that allows our systems, communications and relationship to thrive. Somehow over my lifetime, technology, metrics, efficiency, and external forces have become the louder voices, outshouting our internal knowing and connection. This book serves to help us put things back into balance for the purposes of bringing forth our best leadership for our health and our relationships and of creating the outcomes we want for our families, organizations, communities, and world.

The book lays out simple practices that deepen the roots of your own awareness and clarity and enrich the connections to your deepest knowing, the wisdom of nature. These roots connect us to all life.

And then we can add in and appreciate external metrics, efficiency, and technology.

The activities are simple. There is no magic bullet that hasn't been discussed in different ways for centuries, if not millennia. As I've discovered with my students, however, sometimes things said by another or put in the slightest different way click. That is my hope for you in this book. The practices and steps are simple. The hard thing is the commitment to yourself to allow "the breath before action," to allow yourself the space of connection before running forward, to remember the power of your own knowing before quickly saying yes or no.

This is a book quite simply about awareness and connection. When we give ourselves even a moment of space to deepen into our awareness around us—awareness of how we are feeling, of how others are feeling, of the day, of the weather—it awakens the inner symbiosis of all that we are and allows our ten to twelve physical bodily systems (depending on how you count) to come into harmony in our choices and decision making. It softens the weight we put on the thinking mind (or the mental) to allow the strength and power of the whole self to decide (mind, heart, and bodily systems).

And when we increase our conscious awareness consistently over time, we can't but deepen our connections to self, others, earth, and sky. We hear and listen more closely; we see more widely and more deeply. *As in science, we get into multivariable decision making* that helps us see into the future and understand the implications of our choices. It gets us out of a reliance on short-term satisfaction and helps create roots of long-term joy and thriving. We become the human element in what scientists these days are calling *nonlinear dynamics and complexity science.*

Think about it—imagine sitting down for the next two hours with six or eight random people whom you passed today of different ages, ethnicities, backgrounds, and religions. Together you sat listening to each other's stories about what most impacted your childhoods, and about each other's dreams, hopes, and fears. Imagine just sitting and listening with full presence. Research shows that the connections between you would grow deep and the edges of your righteousness would soften. We learn how to collaborate and come up with more innovative, creative solutions for the betterment of all.

As Ruter Bregman shares in the book *Humankind,* both historical and current data overwhelmingly show that we humans are compassionate, social beings, but turning the tides of systems that were built upon our fears and our belief in human selfishness isn't simple. But it is possible. *Attunement* focuses on small, everyday steps in the practice of living out our deepest values.

And alas, we die. It's a bummer, but it's true. It's the internal contract we made as we entered life on earth. So my hope in writing this guide is that, as we look back from those last moments, whether it's next week or a hundred years from now, we say and feel in our hearts and souls, *Hell, yes! I lived fully. I lived with realness. I lived across all my many roles with the courage to lean into my dreams and my wholeness.* This isn't about life being easy or smooth. Life has waves and bumps and every emotion and experience we can think of. That is life. My goal is to help you connect with that powerful being inside that can ride those waves without being overtaken by them, that can breathe into the bumps and bruises but not get broken or fully twisted by them.

My hope is that, through this guide, you gain insights and practices to allow you to grow your inner clarity and roots of who you deeply are and want to be—to gain the power to dance your dance and to never have to remember what you said because all flows in such alignment with who you are.

Thank you for picking up this book, and I hope we can go together on the journey of daily practices to enliven and re-enchant the full power of who we are as humans living here on this beautiful planet.

1

Beginnings

When I first began contemplating this book, an image kept coming to my mind. The image was of me driving at about eighty miles an hour through all the activities of my days, and every once in a while, in the rearview mirror, I would see someone kindly but persistently trying to get my attention. They might be on a street corner or running behind me and waving, trying to catch up. Occasionally, when I was at a stoplight or stuck in traffic, I'd hear the person's voice a bit louder. I would turn, perhaps to start a conversation, but then the light would turn green or the traffic would begin to move, and on I would go.

And then, the previously unthinkable happened. My car stopped. The spinning world I had known stopped, and I found myself sitting on the couch a lot more than I had in decades. I'd feel that kind yet persistent person often sitting next to me. *Hmm. What to do now?*

Due to COVID-19, many of us were forced to slow down in ways we were quite unaccustomed to and perhaps uncomfortable with. In some moments, we began to feel the expansiveness and power in that quiet, and in other moments, we wanted to scream and jump out of our skins. Our bodies were quite used to the constant movement. We often didn't have to think. We just had to keep moving.

And I realize that reflection time is what *Attunement* is all about. Whether we're zooming all the time at eighty miles an hour or more or we're forced to sit within the confines of our homes, *Attunement* is about helping us develop a powerful dialogue with that person who is in the rearview mirror or sitting next to us. It's about spending a few minutes every day going deeper into the conversation of "What do I make of this one wild and wondrous life of mine? How do I create meaning? What is the meaning I want to create? How do I allow those voices to have a seat at the table, without fear or anger, but with observation and quiet allowance, understanding, and thoughtfulness?"

Attunement shares a simple but profound framework to allow us to deepen and easily connect with that voice within us and create a bridge between our inner relationship and outer experiences of life.

Two Principles of Attunement

Attunement (and the Six Minutes Daily practice) is designed to harness our inner power and help us live thriving lives. It offers practical tools we can use to access our infinite potential and reveals how to do that without depleting our resources. In fact, it expands them. My intention for this book is to help you find better health, stronger relationships, and a thriving, self-empowered future.

It is based on two principles. We have a choice in how we want to show up in this world, and as we become more conscious of our choices, we strengthen our power to build our future. COVID-19 has forced us to take a great pause in our fast-paced, somewhat reactionary lives and look more microscopically at our values. This book is a child of that great pause. It is a simple way for you to *check in with yourself; see how your choices are shifting; and build a powerful, healthy, abundant future for yourself, your business, and* those *you love.*

There is importance in finding balance between our outputs and inputs. The focus falls on our outputs in our culture of action, speed, efficiency, activity, and more. We may even feel that we are addicted to being busy. Perhaps that's why we often say, "How's it going?" instead of "How are you?" While movement isn't a negative thing, it can lead to negative consequences for our health, our relationships, and our thriving, overall success *if we don't find the balance between the amount of energy we exert, externally, and the amount of energy we allow in to refuel ourselves, internally.* This is true for our mental, emotional, physical, creative, and financial energy.

We need only to look at our cultural situation. From our national spending to our individual spending, we are more in debt than ever before. There is a lot of output without enough input. In our physical bodies, adrenal fatigue and autoimmune disorders continue to evolve from diseases rarely heard of forty years ago to nearly epidemic levels now. The biological challenges of *adrenal fatigue* are often referenced as the culprits that are weakening our systems and allowing life-threatening diseases like cancer, heart conditions, and strokes to manifest.

Anxiety, depression, addiction, and suicide rates are at unprecedented levels. We are mentally exhausted. And our creativity, our ability to listen and innovate, is suffering because we are running too fast to juggle all the balls we have in the air with grace.

If you follow *Attunement*'s simple steps (*simple* doesn't mean "easy") and practice consistently over six weeks, you will form new habits that will allow you to be more creative. It is in these quiet shifts that seismic change occurs. This is as true for individuals as it is for families, teams, and organizations. The end result is more aligned, sustainable energy leading to better health outcomes; stronger, trusting relationships; and synergistic teams and organizations. By forming a habit of daily practice of breath, intention, and gratitude, we will learn to expand our thinking and to creatively and thoughtfully respond *rather than impulsively react.* We will take back the reins of our personal life leadership.

How the Six Minutes Daily Practice Began It All

$6 = 3 + 2 + 1$

Allowing ourselves just six minutes a day to quietly check in—three minutes for quiet breath, two for intention setting and reflections based on our core values, and one for a moment of gratitude—changes our trajectory. We begin to make more conscious choices in all areas of our lives—our health, our relationships, at work, and at home. Those choices, no matter how small they may seem, begin to have a synergistic, positive effect.

Six minutes begin to reawaken, realign, and reignite how you want to walk in the world and the difference you will make. Just like brushing our teeth is a daily habit with proven benefits, so too may Six Minutes Daily cleanse the internal layers that limit our light. Six Minutes Daily helps us gain the space to allow our full potential to shine.

The number 6, historically and symbolically, has been thought of as the meeting of heaven and earth (think of the two opposing triangles in a six-pointed star). Done daily (or at least close to daily), the six-minute practice allows us to connect back to ourselves and remember who we are, what's really important, and where we want to go. The key is creating the personal practice to connect to our inner wisdom.

2

Reflections

Light Bulb #1: Leadership is more powerful when it's holistic.

I often can't remember what I ate for breakfast, but I'll never forget a conversation I had more than thirty years ago about the different lenses we use to define success and how they impact our world. It was in the early nineties, only a decade after women really began making their way into management at major companies. Procter & Gamble, the company I began working for right out of college in 1985, still had no women in its highest ranks, let alone in the C-suite of decision makers (CEO, COO, CMO, etc.). It was and still is a promote-from-within company, so it would be another few years before women made it to the higher levels within the organization.

My conversation was with my dear friend Reade Fahs (now the CEO of National Vision, Walmart's eye care centers for nearly twenty years). He and his wife Katie were thinking about having kids, as were my husband and me.

Our conversation went something like this:

Reade: Sandy, I'm envious of women.

Me: And why would that be?

Reade: Because, for the most part, women have a circular, expansive definition of *success*, while men are still too wired for the hunt. Our definition of success is linear, often conditioned by our earliest memories. Success is about climbing the ladder, and when we get to the top, we just create a longer ladder. Women view success from different lenses. It seems women's definition is more about the great balancing act. Yes, women still want and are capable of great financial success, yet they also view children, community, nurturing, health, home, friendships, hobbies, and other parts of life as a huge part of their container of success. And they bring that more holistic view of connection to the workplace. Think of it—for thousands of years, men went out to hunt buffalo while women were in charge of almost everything else. While our worlds have dramatically changed, the ways we define success really haven't. And they need to expand. Capitalism will break otherwise. The ladder can only grow so tall without falling over.

This conversation informs a lot of my work today as an entrepreneurial and leadership coach, consultant, and teacher. In the second part of this guidebook, I share weekly essays and stories to help you practice walking powerfully into effective whole-self leadership, granting the benefits to yourself and to the companies and teams with whom you work.

Companies that practice values-based decision making and have a multifaceted view of success beyond just financials, including the criteria of impact to people (customers, suppliers, and employees) and to the environment, are proving that employees are more loyal with less turnover and absenteeism, customers are more loyal because they trust in the values of the company, and the financial metrics remain strong over the long term.

Light Bulb #2: Success is an inside job.

One recent warm summer night, I sat at a kitchen table for dinner with my four twenty-something-aged sons and their friends. As we chatted, we started a philosophical discussion. I asked them, "What is success?"

"A Lamborghini," one humorously blurted out.

"A lot of money," said someone else.

"Doing a double cork off a cliff," said another, referring to a snowboard trick.

And so it went, full of laughter and fun, as I just listened. Eventually, after many fun activities and acquisitions had been discussed, someone said, "Well, the CEO of Nokia was really successful—that is, until he committed suicide." And the conversation paused.

So I asked, "What does success have to do with happiness?" This is where the conversation became powerful. These educated, thoughtful young men said that, in their experience, our culture puts little value on internal feelings when it comes to success. Throughout all of their education, the focus was on external progress—grades, accomplishments, college acceptance, good jobs, high pay. There was little cultivation or thoughtful discussion about *why*. Bigger must be better. Faster and more were the behaviors that got applauded. They used their fathers' latest focus on multiplying everything they did by ten as an example.

One of them finally said, "I think success in our culture is like a pie-eating contest. The thing is that, if we win, all we get is more pie. So, I guess we better like the pie."

The external outputs are what our culture applauds. The questions then become, *Are we refueling with enough inputs to keep our physical and mental systems thriving? And how do we make sure that pie is actually what fuels us?*

Over the last eight years, I've spent a lot of time reading, learning, and earning advanced degrees in psychology, consciousness, and coaching. I've been blessed to meet some very wise and inspiring people on my journey. One person who has become a powerful mentor to me is psychologist, researcher, and best-selling author Robert Holden.

Here are two of his "light bulbs":

1. When people are asked to choose between success and happiness, fame and happiness, wealth and happiness, power and happiness—over 85% of people choose happiness. And the same is true when we replace the word *happiness* with *love, health,* and *authenticity.*
2. Of all the reliable studies looking for correlations between wealth and happiness, once people are making above the poverty line (about $70,000 for a family), researchers find no correlation between our bank accounts and our sense of happiness.

So why do we keep running faster toward the external goal line to find something that lies within?

In *Six Minutes Daily,* I share stories about my life as a mom of five children, as a former dean and director of career services at Harvard Kennedy School, as a marketing professional, and as an entrepreneur. I have wanted to tell these stories ever since Reade sparked my curiosity thirty-five years ago.

In that time, I've seen how taking a whole-self-leadership approach to work-life balance and how we define success builds health, connections, and abundance for individuals and organizations collectively. Adopting this broader view of leadership begins with understanding and practicing attunement. Now that our country is facing unprecedented challenges across many areas (politics, pandemic, guns, women's rights, mental health, and democracy itself), I am compelled to share this learning more than ever.

The linear drive for success can and needs to be balanced with an expansive, interconnected, circular view of success—incorporating our own physical, emotional, and mental health; the health of the earth; and the health of our communities—as important components of both short- and long-term success. Our survival depends on it.

3

Key Reflection Questions for Journaling

Attunement helps develop your commitment to a practice that will grow, strengthen, and awaken your powerful potential. It reconnects you with your deepest, authentic, radiant self while you learn to consciously release the layers of some of your past experiences that have begun to harden into concrete instead of flowing to let in more light, creativity, and expansiveness.

As part of this work, I use three essential questions to consistently guide my practice and my work with others. They are questions without finite, closed answers that you can revisit over your lifetime to continue to expand your awareness, refine your clarity, and support you as you walk into the life you dream. Life is far from fair. It is easy to fall into victimhood and give away our power. A key phrase to bring our power back to ourselves relates to recognizing victimhood as a trap. Circumstances aren't happening to us; they are helping us define who we are and how we show up and asking us if we want to grow. It is how we choose to deal with these circumstances that allows the real learning to begin.

Three Essential Questions

1. How do I define success?
2. Where and how do I get my energy?
3. How do I choose to spend my time?

Question 1: How do I define success?

What does success look like for you? So often, we get up and start running without asking ourselves this basic question. And I don't mean, *What do you want for breakfast or dinner tonight?* although those small questions are important. I mean, What do you want your life to look like? What values do you want to embody in the steps you take?

An intentional life requires thought, focus, and tough choices. And yes, it takes sacrifice. Even sacrifices can be joyful when we know why we're making them. I write these words at five thirty in the morning. A large part of me would still love to be sleeping. Yet, because I chose to get up, these words arrive. I now have the joy of watching as the world moves from darkness to light. I thank the coming dawn. Getting up early was a worthy sacrifice of sleep.

As you navigate this book, you will notice that I ask this question a lot: How do you describe success? What does it feel like? Look like? It is important to define this for yourself. Your answers should evolve, but the values that underlie your definition of success may remain consistent. The more you consider and define who you are and how you want to show up before focusing on exactly what you are doing or the external definition of success, the more choices will present themselves. If you know your *why*, your *what* becomes less important. Many paths lead there.

The answers begin with reflection. They evolve when we allow a few moments of space on a consistent basis. The first step is to ask quietly and be patient enough to listen for the answer. Chances are that the answer won't be some grand epiphany; it will be subtle, reinforcing the importance of listening.

This act of becoming takes conscious effort. I hope you do this work for yourself. The world needs you. It needs your conscious understanding of who you are, who you want to be, and how you can best bring your gifts to the world.

Someone once told me that, among the billions of stars in the galaxy, there is a star as individual as each of us, guiding us back to ourselves. That star can't be found in Facebook posts, Twitter feeds, Instagram tags, or any material wealth. Even enormous wealth won't feed that deeper longing to be authentically you.

It's hard to find the star that helps you answer this existential question: How do you define success? It's hard to change habits when you are pulled and pushed by the external forces of this world. That is why I continue to ask the same question and allow the answers to slowly grow roots of awareness. *Quiet shift; seismic change.*

Question 2: Where and how do I get my energy?

I've observed hundreds of people (beginning with myself) over the last thirty years in leadership, marketing, and entrepreneurship roles self-sabotage their dreams or walk away from huge opportunities because of one thing—internal fear. This fear, in the form of believing you aren't good enough or deserving enough, is an insidious fog that can creep into everything. This fog of fear can undermine confidence, health, and your sense of worth. Fear is like a dark tunnel that, often, only semi-consciously has us doing all sorts of contortions to avoid it.

Going around it only makes the black hole of internal fear grow. As we learn to face it, walk through it, talk to it, and learn from it, it begins to lighten and may even eventually disappear. We begin to light up the tunnel.

Making fear release its paralyzing grip is not a mental exercise. We can't out analyze it. We can't strategize it away. In our current rational world, fear doesn't care. In fact, most of the time, we aren't even consciously aware that inner fear is driving our decisions.

One way to release fear is breathing in and out through our hearts—breathing in the values we want to live by—ultimately to breathe in love. Just try it. Think of something that brings up internal fear or anxiety, something that causes your body to tighten or constrict. Now, close your eyes and focus on breathing directly from your heart. Focus on something you love. Focus on allowing love to flood through you, and it doesn't matter from where (Spirit, stars, the earth, someone special, a pet.... Just allow the feeling to grow within you). Do you feel your body relax, even just for a second? And in that second of expansion, you also begin to engage the incredible systems of your body (nervous, endocrine, adrenal, respiratory, etc.) to get out of flight-or-fight mode and access to a far deeper power within you. Connecting with that inner source that is beyond your analytical mind helps you observe your situation from varying vantage points and develop new ways to respond. Tapping into this more heart- and core-oriented energy allows you to pause, to reflect, and to problem solve in innovative, creative ways. You begin to see interconnections of actions and respond from a place that isn't just an immediate reaction.

This kind of energy shift is our greatest superpower in expanding our spheres of what we can control. We can't control outside events to a great extent. But we can control how we respond to those events. And in that shift is the magic that opens many new paths of opportunity and choice.

Gaining More Energy

Grit. Resilience. Persistence. Stickiness. These are all incredibly important traits for growth, success, and achievement. These traits make the difference in almost everything we pursue. Can we get up and go even when the chips are down, the morning is cold and rainy, or enticing distraction is within reach? Developing and maintaining the discipline and internal capacity for some discomfort and angst as we continue walking forward is extremely important.

All of that grit and resilience takes energy. I can almost feel it as I write this—the contracting of my muscles against going forward. So, another question I may repeat is, "What is the source of my energy, and how can I replenish it over time?"

So often, in our fast-paced, go-go-go culture, we seem to get that energy from a limited and not easily regenerated source—caffeine, adrenaline, even drugs. Our bodies get addicted to the jolt of a pick-me-up. We even come to believe that the adrenaline burst makes us better. Fear motivates us to do the extraordinary—dodge a speeding train or sprint the last mile in a race—but it doesn't always work well on a daily basis when we need to get through our to-do lists. Our human biology doesn't work that way.

Living on adrenaline depletes our systems in the long run. Just as caffeine dehydrates us, adrenaline prevents our energy from creating other needed hormones that provide long-term balance and health to our main bodily systems (digestive, nervous, circulatory, endocrine, skeletal, lymphatic, immune, integumentary, urinary, cardiovascular, respiratory, muscular, reproductive, etc.).

Adrenaline also awakens the follow-up hormone cortisol, which keeps us alert to danger or threats even after the initial rush of adrenaline has left. Cortisol keeps us on edge, sometimes giving us the extra "zing" or persistence to push ahead. But what if there is no imminent threat to our safety, or even worse, what if we've trained our bodies to think that an interaction with someone or something different is a threat? Our bodies may become so used to living in that fear-based reality that we even begin to constrict physically, unconsciously contracting to protect our hearts.

Adrenaline and cortisol push energy to our limbs, taking it away from our vital organs—including the brain and heart—to fuel our arms and legs for fight or flight. As our vision narrows, our fears about safety become more profound.

While the body exerts more energy for fight or flight, the feel-good hormones oxytocin and serotonin, which allow us to think creatively and find solutions, may be depleted. By training our bodies to pull from the well of hormones that narrow our view and constrict our vision, we are robbing ourselves of feeling peace, trust, connection, and joy.

By committing to the daily practice of breathing in our values, expanding into our hearts, setting intentions, and expressing gratitude, we begin to pull energy back to our cores, to our vital organs, to our hearts, freeing up more feel-good hormones that allow us to come back home to ourselves, to even more deeply appreciate the present moment, and to expand our choices and decision making.

Question 3: How do I choose to spend my time?

Time is our most precious asset; our choice of how to use it impacts everything. Somehow, during our lifetimes, it feels like we have lost control of time. Instead of our choosing how we use time, it often drives us. We wake up feeling behind. We go to bed tired, wishing we had more time, and the same feeling repeats itself day after day.

This feeling of not having enough time can lead to many negative outcomes to our health, our relationships, our success, and our futures.

Six Minutes Daily can retrain us on how to use our time with clarity, confidence, and courage to make decisions for ourselves, our families, and our organizations based on our core values. Try the sample practice below to quietly begin seeing *time as your asset* to help you realize your vision and goals.

Allow yourself to balance your time with another kind of energy to help inspire your vision, tenacity, and resilience. Allow your deep well of inner wisdom and knowing to constantly be replenished. As we slow down for a few minutes daily, we begin to refuel and expand our vision, space, and powerful internal health systems and hormones, giving us creative strength for the long-term marathon of life.

Six Minutes Daily Overview

1. A few minutes of breathing in a core value
2. A couple of minutes of daily intention setting for how we want to show up in our day
3. A minute of breathing in and feeling gratitud

Do you have six minutes?

Begin the shift with this simple guided practice. Sit down right now, wherever you are. Take a deep breath. Allow the light from the sun to filter down through the crown of your head and into your body. Allow the fire from deep below the earth's crust to rise up through your feet and meet the sunlight at your heart. Allow your body to be held by the earth below you. Drop your shoulders, loosen your hips, and relax your feet. Gently ask your heart to open to all of this light and fire—not from caffeine or adrenaline but from a power of your own. Spend a few minutes here asking for expansion and space. As you breathe in and out, try to breathe through your nose. Focus on a word or a key value you want to remember today as you step into the world, reinforcing how you want to show up and what you want to embody. Slowly close your eyes and deepen into your breath.

As you come back, allow yourself to write down some intentions, ideally beginning with "I am" followed by an active tense verb: *I am listening deeply before responding. I am pausing before saying yes. I am interrupting my inner critic and shifting my inner voice to creatively reinforce my value and provide empowering thoughts and ways of being.*

Last, spend a minute writing down someone or something for which you are grateful. As you write, allow your thoughts to flow down to your core, expanding your feelings of joy and appreciation.

And repeat this daily. Need inspiration? Visit the fifty-two-week practice guide of daily exercises at the end of this book. Follow your own compass and retrain your brain to take back control of your time.

4

The Six Practices of Attunement for Authentic, Deepened Leadership

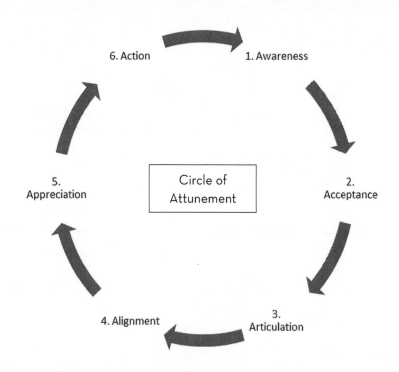

6. Action

1. Awareness

5. Appreciation

Circle of Attunement

2. Acceptance

4. Alignment

3. Articulation

Practice 1: Awareness
of Our Choices

W e start making choices the moment we open our eyes to the new day. Do we get out of bed? What do we do next? How do we greet those we see? And so on. Choices define how we decide to use our time, and they define how we show up in our relationships.

Thus, the first lesson in our attunement practice is simply to acknowledge that we have a choice in what we do and how we do it. There's a saying in psychology: The issue isn't the issue. It's how we choose to deal with the issue that's the issue.

This awareness of choice means that we are taking responsibility for our behaviors and our actions. It means that we are choosing not to give away our power by falling into victim mode or blaming external factors. This doesn't mean that we are bypassing our emotions or feelings. It is important to recognize and allow the emotions. *Awareness* means that we don't have to be swept away by our feelings and just react based on those feelings.

Awareness of choice means that we allow ourselves to pause for a moment before we respond, before we make a choice. This pause provides us the space to reflect and connect back to who we want to be and why.

Think about it. Where in your day today have you quickly reacted without pause? In doing that, some of us may fall into saying yes before we even know what we've committed to, later causing exhaustion and internal frustration at our lack of boundaries and priorities. Others may get triggered and react in anger or defensively, putting up barriers to communication that weren't intended and are detrimental to building stronger, trusting relationships.

Awareness of choice also means that we begin to better own our time. What are our goals and our priorities? How are we choosing to spend our time in achieving those goals?

How often do we hear and say, "I'm too busy. I don't have time. I wish I had more time." But the funny thing is that we all have the same amount of time. As we build our awareness and ownership around choice, we begin to take back our time instead of chasing it.

Here's the deal with the Six Minutes Daily practice: We start small. Today, the only responsibility you have is to build your awareness muscle and open your eyes just a smidge wider.

Are you aware, when you get out of bed, why you chose to get out of bed? In that awareness, can you take even a second to thank yourself for your choice?

Part of our work in expanding our awareness is to be kinder to ourselves. This work isn't about letting our internal voices have a heyday in reminding us of all the things we don't do right. Building our awareness helps us realize that we are much more than those often incessant, judgmental, frightened, or angry voices inside us that sound so critical because they think that, by keeping us small, they are keeping us safe. They forget that we are not three or ten years old anymore. They forget that we have grown up and can handle far more than we could when we were young.

Building our awareness muscles also means we can see that inner voice for what it is and know that it is not the full definition of who we are. We can choose to say thank you to the voice and send it to Tahiti for an extended vacation.

Today's work is just to take a few minutes to become more aware of what we are feeling and of the choices we are making.

Six Questions About Awareness

1. Do you believe you have a choice in how you show up? Reflect on your answer and why.
2. What are you feeling right now? List any emotions, thoughts, or feelings without any judgment.

3. Now, scan your body—what are you aware of? Where may you be holding something? What does it feel like just to observe it?

4. Can you think of an experience you had today in which a pause of awareness may have shifted the outcome? Describe what happened. Describe the choice you made and a choice you'd like to make next time.

5. What fears, emotions, or internal voices come up when you think about that different choice?

6. What commitments can you make to allow your awareness to flow?

This work is all about consistent practice. Expanding our awareness isn't any different than learning to play the piano or kick a soccer ball. The more we practice the pause and check in with our awareness before we act or make a decision, the more our awareness and clarity will grow. We will own our choices and how we choose to use that most important of assets, our time. This is about expanding our potential and building our sense of personal leadership. It is about slowing down for a second to speed up for the long run.

Patterns

One more piece about expanding our awareness—we all have internal patterns. Just like most of us are left-handed or right-handed, we also have patterns around how we organize, prioritize, make decisions, make choices, find our sense of security and belonging, and so on. By the time we are five years old, we have created internal road maps for how to navigate the world and how to find safety, acceptance, belonging, and love. Some of these internal road maps may be hard wired from birth, and some are developed based on circumstances. It is the dance between nature and nurture as our brain develops in those early years (and neuroscientists say that about 75 percent of brain development occurs in the first two years) that creates these patterns. Patterns help us become more efficient so we can get more done. What if we had to think through how to walk every time we stood up? Thankfully, muscles develop memories and patterns to allow us to do those things that are rote without using too much energy.

The key to being aware of our patterns is becoming aware of our abilities to shift them. Many of those behavioral patterns were created when we were young, without much experience. As adults, life may be very different, and our coping skills are much more developed. By expanding our awareness, we begin to observe our patterns and learn to consciously use them or not instead of just being unconsciously driven by them.

If you are interested in learning more about the patterns that might drive you, many highly valid and reliable assessment tools are available, like the Myers-Briggs Type Indicator and the Enneagram. The key is to realize that there are no right or wrong answers. These assessments do not define us; they simply identify patterns. As we develop an awareness of and perhaps the language around the pattern, we may hold them less tightly. We may find humor in understanding some of our behaviors. We may take certain behaviors of others less personally, and we may also begin to understand that people we care for are not necessarily doing things that hurt or bother us. This awareness around patterns can also give us language to discuss our differences—again, without making something right or wrong.

As we begin to expand our awareness and understand when and how we might break out of old patterns to tap into our deeper potential, we add more arrows of choice to our quiver of opportunities.

Learning More about Enneagram & MBTI Patterns

If you Google *enneagram*, you will find many links to assessments and books. The Enneagram Institute assessment and the book *The Wisdom of the Enneagram* by Don Riso and Russ Hudson are helpful places to start in understanding the strengths and pitfalls of our styles and type preferences.

Many assessments are available on the web for the Myers-Briggs Type Indicator. A book I often use in to help clients gain insights into preferences and type is *Please Understand Me* by David Keirsey and Marilyn Bates.

Practice 2: Acceptance

What would it, could it, or does it feel like to sit here, slow down, and just breathe in the *acceptance* that you are worthy, that you are enough, and that you are loved—deeply.

As you roll your eyes, back away, and find reasons to throw this book out the window, please first just sit and take a minute to breathe peace, love, and light into every cell in your being. Allow them to flow like a warm, sparkling river down through the crown of your head; through your shoulders and arms; down through your heart, your core; into your hips, thighs, knees, and ankles; around your feet; and out into the ground. And through those channels, visualize the stream eventually flowing down through the bottoms of your feet deep into the earth. Allow yourself to release any unwanted energies, patterns, shadows, constrictions, feelings, and gunk into the stream flowing through your being, and allow those energies to flow down into the fires of the earth's core. Visualize the ashes becoming mulch, filled with the earth's nutrients and forever released from the tension inside your body.

Then, through the canals carved from your feet to the core, visualize the warmth and nurturing of Mother Earth rising up through the bottom of your feet, up your calves and legs, and into your core. Allow this light and fire to swirl into every crevice of your being, illuminating all with the power of acceptance of your wholeness and the connection and love from the earth and the sky.

This exercise isn't about doing. It is about being. It is about remembering and allowing your deeper knowing to come forth with compassion and courage to remind you that you are so worthy—in the quiet and peace of this moment and always.

And this exercise is just the opposite of narcissism. Narcissism rises out of insecurity that leads people to project how great they are to the world, creating a reflection and self-image that seems to just be about them.

Acceptance asks you to look deeper into your being. It asks

us to remember, feel, and see our younger selves, filled with hope and innocence and love. When we find and reconnect with those beings deep within us, we soften. We allow that fullness of love to come forth. It can take time, but it is extremely healing. It brings all the parts of us home to our hearts and cores. It also allows us to begin releasing self-judgments. This softening has a courageous layer underneath that helps us become open and more vulnerable in a positive sense. We learn the power of our being within us, so we no longer need to wear the armor of protection and distance in our outer layers.

Clients and students sometimes ask if doing this work will make them weak or lazy—if by accepting themselves they will lose their drive. They wonder at the beginning if they will end up not caring for much and just sit staring at the clouds or playing video games. Actually, just the opposite occurs. As we practice the power of acceptance of our goodness, worthiness, and lovability, our inner fire grows. Ideas, creativity, and passions around our purpose grow stronger roots.

We no longer need to prove anything to someone else or the world. We lean into our dreams and let go of our baggage. An energy rises just like in the childhood story of the little engine that could.

The Other Side of Acceptance

There's another side to acceptance, and that side goes hand in hand with forgiveness. Here's my story of this side of acceptance that forever shifted my life. When I was twenty-one and just about to graduate from college, my fifty-two-year-old dad went into an alcohol-induced coma from which he would never wake up. My freshman-year roommate and dear friend died by suicide, and my only living grandparent (my dad's mother) died of a broken heart – all within a few week period. As an only child, my small family became much smaller in an instant.

I felt numb and heartbroken. After graduation, I was to begin a job in brand management at Procter & Gamble. I was told it was a great opportunity, so I went through the motions of moving to Cincinnati, setting up my first apartment, and walking into the corporate world. I tried to create a wall of armor around my pain, but our bodies don't work that way. No matter how hard I tried to push away the emotions and grief, the dark shadows remained.

Then one day, a friend gave me Scott Peck's book, *The Road Less Traveled*. I remember nothing about the book besides the first page or so, but that page shifted everything. It said something like, *If you think life is supposed to always be easy and full of sunshine, you are going to spend half your life disappointed. But if you understand and accept that life has ups and downs, good days and hard days, you'll be grateful for the good days and ready for the more challenging ones.*

This is the other side of acceptance—to hold life as a big container of everything without getting stuck in blaming, anger, and victimhood. Again, it doesn't mean we do an emotional bypass of all of our feelings. It does mean that we don't allow the hard days to become the lens through which we see the world.

I often work with clients who hold disappointments, losses, or betrayals deep in their being years after the event. Their anger can become visceral. And the question becomes, "Whom is that anger serving?" The rest of the world has moved on. What would it feel like to accept that it happened and even forgive such that it no longer holds you back or limits your energy?

This kind of acceptance is challenging, I know. I can hear the *yeah, but*s right now. Another perspective on this kind of acceptance comes from Viktor Frankl in his landmark book, *Man's Search for Meaning*. Frankl was a survivor of a German concentration camp during the Holocaust who went on to become a psychiatrist. His insight gained through observing human behavior in the most horrific and barbaric of circumstances was the following: Some people continued to carry light, kindness, and grace even as they knew they were soon to die. When he asked them how they maintained such an attitude and demeanor, their answers came down to this: Others can take away everything material from me, but they cannot take from me how I choose to show up and how I derive meaning from life.

When we practice acceptance and forgiveness, we maintain our own sense of power and inner strength. No one can take that away. And in that acceptance of our own light within the kaleidoscope of life experiences, we gain the power of our deepest potential. We learn the true meaning of courage—power from the heart.

Key Questions to Ask Yourself

1. What comes up when you breathe in acceptance of your own wholeness and worthiness?
2. How does it feel to accept yourself as enough?
3. Where and toward whom are you holding any sadness or anger?
4. How does it feel to accept those events as part of your past and forgive? (Some key sentences that may help include these: I forgive _____ for _____ for I will no longer allow this energy to hold me back from my dreams and potential; I forgive myself for judging myself as _____ for the truth is that I was doing the best that I could at the time; and I forgive myself for buying into the conception that _____ for the truth is that life holds many moments.

Practice 3: Articulation
of Who We Are and How We Want to Show Up

Articulation is the opportunity to clarify our awareness and best describe the acceptance of the remarkable beings that we are. What vision, definition of success, or list of values do we use as our foundation from which to build our lives? Who do we want to be? What do we want to stand for? When we look backward, what do we want to be remembered for? As we practice, we develop clarity around those answers, and our decision making becomes easier. We continually pause to check in with ourselves, expanding our self-trust. It's not about being perfect—it's about the gentle, unfolding clarity of our own value.

The important part of the exercises below, designed to help us define our core values, vision, and purpose, is to realize that each of us is one person who plays many roles. We are not many different people.

Trust is a core component in strengthening our health, building our relationships, and opening up to the synergy and synchronicity of life success. If we behave one way at work, a different way in sports, and yet a different way at home with our partners or families, it's hard for us to have trust in ourselves, let alone gain others' trust. Nobody can be sure who's going to show up. Over time, that uncertainty constricts possibility. It doesn't expand our potential.

This isn't to say that we might not have secondary behaviors that are slightly more formal, organized, or spontaneous at different times on different days. But when we embody the handful of core values that consistently drive our decision making and behaviors, internal trust grows and the web of trusting relationships all around us expands. The philosopher Goethe explained this flow as "all things moving in our favor both seen and unseen."

Values Exercise

Using the list below, circle ten values that you see as important in defining who you are and how you want to show up in the world. These words do not have to be fully true right now. They can be aspirational.

Now, cut out five of the words.

Next, write down your top three words in the box on this page as well as on three sticky notes. These are the values that speak to you as the deepest roots of your foundation or that represent fundamentally who you want to be in every role that you play in life—as a friend, professional, family member, parent, child, community member, spiritual member, hobbyist, home creator, and so on.

1. Put one sticky note on your bathroom mirror.
2. Put the second on your computer or desk.
3. Put the third on your dashboard of your car.

Finally, use these words in all three parts of your Six Minutes Daily practice: three minutes of quiet breath, two minutes of positive intentions, and one minute of gratitude.

Reflect on these words each day for the next three to four weeks. How do they speak to you? Do they inspire you? Is something missing? How do you define each word for yourself? Keep a pad and pen nearby or use a voice recorder on your phone to capture your thoughts. If there's a word missing or a better word that arises, allow yourself to optimize your core words.

It may sound crazy, but just the act of bringing these words to your consciousness begins a shift. Articulating these values will inevitably increase your awareness and allow you to pause before your respond. Step by step, you walk into the person you know yourself to be.

The shift may be rather quiet and incremental. Rarely is the shift a biblical, sea-parting one, but we believe wholeheartedly that it will come. As David Whyte says in his poem "The Truelove," "subtly and intimately in the face of the one you know you have to love." Accept that that person is *you,* and abundance will come.

Sandy Schultz

Define Your Values

First circle ten. If you do not see a word or idea that's important to you, please feel free to write it in.

Accountable	Excellent	Perfect
Accurate	Excited	Pious
Achiever	Expert	Positive
Adventurous	Explorer	Practical
Altruistic	Expressive	Prepared
Ambitious	Fair	Professional
Assertive	Faithful	Prudent
Balanced	Family-oriented	Quality-oriented
Being the best	Fit	Reliable
Belonging	Fluent	Resourceful
Bold	Focused	Restrained
Calm	Free	Results-oriented
Careful	Fun	Rigorous
Challenger	Generous	Security-focused
Cheerful	Goodness	Self-actualized
Clear-minded	Grace	Self-controlled
Committed	Growth-oriented	Selfless
Community-oriented	Happy	Self-reliant
Compassionate	Hard worker	Sensitive

Competitive	Health-oriented	Serene/peaceful
Consistent	Helping society	Service-oriented
Content	Holy	Shrewd
Continuous improver	Honest	Simplicity-focused
Contributor	Honorable	Soundness-focused
Controller	Humility	Speedy/agile
Cooperative	Independent	Spontaneous
Correct	Ingenious	Stable
Courteous	Inner harmony	Strategic
Creative	Inquisitive	Strong
Curious	Insightful	Structured
Decisive	Intelligent	Successful
Democratic	Intellectual	Supportive
Dependable	Intuitive	Teamwork-oriented
Determined	Joyful	Temperate
Devout	Justice-minded	Thankful
Diligent	Leadership oriented	Thorough
Disciplined	Legacy	Thoughtful
Discrete	Love	Timely
Diverse	Loyal	Tolerant
Dynamic	Making a difference	Traditional
Economical	Mastery-minded	Trustworthy
Effective	Merit-minded	Truth-seeking
Efficient	Obedient	Understanding
Elegant	Open	Unique
Empathetic	Organized	Unity-oriented
Enjoyer of life	Original	Useful
Enthusiastic	Patriotic	Visionary
Equality-minded		Vitality-minded

Now cross out five, leaving you with five words or core values reflecting how you would like to be described over your lifetime. Perhaps they will be the common threads when people from all parts of your life give speeches at your ninetieth birthday celebration.

Finally, see if you can remove two more—giving you the top three values that are important to you in the description of who you are.

Vision

A second powerful tool in articulating your values is to allow yourself to hypothetically look backward from the end or latter part of your life. Write your retirement speech or even the eulogy that you would like someone to say or write for you. What difference did your life make to others? How did you live your life? What did you accomplish? What will you be remembered for? What was the definition of success that drove you? What do you want others to feel when they remember you?

Write this speech in the *present tense* looking backwards and write with as much color and description as you can. Write it as your ideal scene. *It does not have to be completely true right now.* Write it in the positive, not the nonnegative—meaning lean in to how you want to show up and have relationships with others when you look back. Don't' write about what you don't want. Write about what you do want, and write it as true *in the present tense.* As an example, a sentence about relationships with family members might be, "Sandy opened her heart to others with patience, compassion, and clarity. She taught others how to have clear boundaries and compassionate listening," the negative converse of which would be something like, "Sandy didn't get triggered by others' reactiveness."

Again, allow yourself to write without judgment (especially self-judgment). This speech isn't about what's perfectly true right now. It is about what calls to you inside and what you aspire to be. Allowing that deeper voice to gain strength through the power of your words opens a door to possibility. It allows us to begin walking forward with our eyes a bit wider, with our conscious knowing a bit clearer. And as we grow in our awareness of what we want and how we want to show up, small shifts begin to occur. We may see a new possibility or hear a different voice inside, helping us in our decision making.

Writing this vision looking backward is an exercise you might want to do annually after rereading it weekly or monthly and allowing it to grow and unfold. What else occurs to you? What is missing? What has changed? This work is like exercising a muscle—it takes practice. It needs to stay flexible and fluid. When we allow this inner voice to be creative, authentic, and honest, it will grow in confidence.

I often use my sons' experience with snowboarding as an analogy. When they were small, they decided they wanted to be pro snowboarders. So, when they were eight, six, and five, Santa brought the whole family (including Mom and Dad) snowboards. We used to spend many weekends at Stratton Mountain in Vermont and attend the annual snowboarding national competition each spring. My sons dreamt of Shaun White flying off sixty-foot jumps as they strapped on their snowboards, which were the size of skateboards, and learned to balance going down the bunny hills. An inch or two of air was cause for celebration. Year after year, they practiced. With inches growing to feet, they soared off bigger and bigger jumps on the mountain. In time, one became Olympic bound, and another came in sixth in the junior national competition. Now in their twenties, they carve and soar with the grace of flight on the mountain, and it all began with the vision of where they wanted to be in a decade, not where they began. They continued to see beyond the bumps, bruises, and broken bones to help their vision become reality.

Our life vision is no different. If we learn to lean into our vision of how we want to live and why and what brings us joy, connection, and love, the abundance comes. And remember, money is just a commodity. It is a means to a goal, but what is the goal? If money is the primary goal, without the consciousness of who we uniquely are and desire to be, our light dims. Our potential constricts. The door starts to close on our deepest desire and knowing.

And what can happen if we feel that sense of frustration, anger, and loss of dreams? We may take it out on ourselves, listening to our inner critics that like to tell us all the things we don't do well; we may begin to muffle those inner voices through behaviors that don't fully serve us—becoming too busy, overeating, using drugs or alcohol to find some peace; or we may project those feelings of frustration onto others, blaming them for our lack of opportunity or success.

That is when the layers of mud covering our dreams become thicker and heavier. And with that awareness and our individual commitment to articulating what calls, those layers of mud begin to wash away. Your daily practice of breathing in that vision or setting a small intention for the day to move that vision forward into reality is like a warm spring rain, clearing away the winter's cold and opening you up to your remembering.

This practice of writing your living vision can even be done for a shorter time period, like two or three years from now. Practice with both—looking backward over a lifetime and looking backward from just a few years from now. *In every case, write this narrative in the present tense.* And then do it again. Read it aloud to yourself. How deeply can you breathe in your words and thoughts? How does your body feel? Reflect on your inner knowing and awareness.

> **Retirement speech:** Get out a piece of paper or journal and just allow the flow of writing. And then tomorrow, do it again.
>
> **Living vision three years from now:** "I wake up on (insert date three years from now), I look around." Now write what you're seeing, thinking about, doing today, and remembering from yesterday. Allow

yourself to have joy and abundance in whatever way that means to you.

Purpose

The last exercise of self-articulation involves purpose. I use purpose work as a way to articulate in a phrase or a sentence why you are here. It provides another way to bring you home to your own deeper power. In Nick Craig's book *Leading from Purpose*, he explains that, when we find that deeper *why*, our focus on what we are doing becomes secondary. Like the values exercise, we bring a clearer awareness to why and how we show up, and then great things begin to happen.

Here, I use the analogy of a story I heard years ago on National Public Radio (NPR) about a gurney attendant at Massachusetts General Hospital. He was the person who would pick people up from their hospital rooms and transport them to the operating room. And he loved to sing. Seeing that people were often nervous and afraid, he'd use his singing to help calm their nerves as he moved them down the halls of the hospital. He learned hundreds of songs. People smiled as he shared his gift. In the NPR interview, he said he felt like he was the luckiest man around to be able to bring joy to others. Some would consider his job to be manual labor, but he brought his purpose of sharing joy through music to his job and, thus, elevated everyone. That is living one's purpose.

Simon Sinek's TED Talk "The Golden Circle" further reinforces this point. He talks about the passion of the Wright brothers and explains why Apple can successfully play in many product categories while other computer companies have failed.

How do you begin to uncover your purpose? Here are three simple questions to begin the process.

1. Can you remember a joyful childhood experience or experiences where you just felt in the flow? Explain the

memory, the feelings, and write down the thoughts that come with that memory.

2. Think of a pivotal moment in your life (Craig calls them "crucible moments") when something very challenging happened. How did you handle it? What personal resources or strengths did you use to overcome that challenge?

3. If you walked away from all the things you're currently involved in, what would people miss about your being there? This is not a time to be humble. Allow yourself to breathe in your goodness, your strengths, and your specialness.

4. Now, as you reflect on the answers to those three questions, what comes to mind when you're asked to write a sentence about why you're here and what your purpose is? Be playful. This is your sentence. Allow it to resonate to you.

Values, vision, and purpose are the three legs of your personal articulation stool. They can grow and change; however, the important piece is that you practice them in your flow of life. Whether you put them on sticky notes on your bathroom mirror, computer, and steering wheel or write them on a pad at your bedside, create a practice that allows you to remain aware of what you wrote. Take time every week to reflect on, improve, and expand this language. The more aware you are of them, the more they will deepen into your muscle memory, thought process, and decision making.

This may seem ridiculously analytical, but these ideas have the ability to expand your world and quietly shift the potential of who you are and how you show up in the world.

Practice 4: Alignment
Across the Many Roles of Our Sunshine Ball

The Roles We Play

How do you embody your core values in your different roles? Where is it easy? Where is it harder? What can you learn from that awareness?

*Long term - why did we choose to live this life?
What difference did we want to make?

Life is a journey, not a destination. No shoulds.

Okay, so now we have some awareness of our ability to choose how we show up, we're breathing in acceptance of all that's come before and our own wholeness, and we've begun to articulate what it is we want to stand for and be remembered for and why.

The next step is to begin understanding how this work plays out in all of the different roles we play. As I've said, we may play many roles (as shown above), but each of us is still only one person. Those who choose to put on incredibly different hats when they show up in different roles are, at best, thought of with some unease and skepticism, as we have little trust that we know who they really are. At worst, they are deemed to have a significant personality disorder.

Again, I am not saying that there aren't many beautiful aspects to all of us, and we can all put on more professional faces and more goofy, spontaneous ones. However, underneath the cloaks we wear, it's important to have clarity around the core values that ignite and run our engines.

And in our growing awareness and clarity, certain roles may fully embrace our core values or at least some of them—where we feel in flow and at ease with that deeper part of us. And we may play other roles in which we feel like those core values, purposes, and visions can't be brought forth, as they wouldn't be appreciated or useful.

In this awareness lies our opportunity for growth. When we feel a need to sidestep or ignore who we want to be or how we want to bring our best to the world, it's like cutting off a limb of ourselves in how we show up. We put an obstacle in our paths, limiting our internal powerful energy from easily flowing.

A simple exercise, just to practice your growing internal alignment, is to write all of your potential roles in life (friend, sibling, parent, partner, professional, athlete, homemaker, hobbyist, adventurer, community member, spiritual being, etc.) on spokes extending from a circle and then write your core values in the middle of the circle, as demonstrated above. By each role, rate yourself on a scale of one to ten showing how well you are bringing that value to your life in that role (ten means you are fully embodying the value; one means you're not embodying it much at all).

In roles where you give yourself an eight, nine, or ten, reflect on why.

1. What feels good?
2. What makes it easy?

3. What are some examples of when you felt greatly in alignment?
4. Can you write down some reflections to help you deepen into that knowing, feeling, and awareness?
5. Which roles do you rate at eight or higher?
6. What reflections do you have about how this feels?

Now reflect on roles where you rate yourself a five or lower on one of your core values.

7. Why?
8. What insights come to mind?

Remember, this reflection and work is without judgment. We are just learning to observe and investigate. If that inner voice of criticism or weight comes up, close your eyes and kindly ask it to go somewhere else. You have powerful work to do right now, and you don't need that voice bogging you down. The more you can become aware of that voice and the weight associated with it, the more you can consistently and gently separate from the voice and send it to another chair or to Tahiti—a place where you can speak with it and observe it from a distance.

As you observe places and roles where your values aren't as strong, think to yourself, *What is a small way that I can better bring that value to life in that role this week?* It need not be big or dramatic. It's about the small steps.

A great example is a client I once worked with who was a hotel manager. When she listed her values and purpose in her vision work, she talked about how important it was to give back and how her purpose was to help sick children—although she felt she had no room to do much of that in her current, very busy and intense professional role. In defining some small steps and goals, we developed a plan for her to work with the Make-a-Wish Foundation to find a child who wanted to stay in the area where she managed the hotel and have a dream come true. This aligned her professional success with her values and vision. For a few minutes every week, she worked on this plan, and everything began to spiral up. Her energy and joy in her work improved, the publicity behind this work helped the hotel thrive, and some children's dreams came true. Health, relationships, and abundance all grew.

In another example, a client listed faith as one of her core values but felt she couldn't bring that to her workplace. We talked about how she defined faith (compassion, kindness, trust, love) and identified small steps that helped her internalize how she could indeed bring faith into her professional life.

Small steps to aligning who we are and how we want to show up with what we do in all our roles can lead to a seismic shift in our inner clarity, confidence, and competence so that we can bring all we are to the world—and in that alignment, synergy happens. Things we never expected or thought of occur. Serendipity and synchronicity become more frequent. Perhaps you could make a practice of writing down synchronicities, or happy coincidences. The more you become aware of them, the more they happen.

Practice 5: Appreciation
Breathing in Gratitude for Even the Smallest Things

The fifth step in our building blocks of attunement is about appreciation. What does it feel like to daily and consistently deepen your sense of gratitude for even just waking up in the morning (as my ninety-year-old mother likes to say)? Yes, there may be a lot in our lives to feel frustrated about; however, if we choose to focus just on the frustrations, we reduce our internal power. We constrict our energy and limit our focus. It is not good for our health or our problem-solving abilities. If we remind ourselves and breathe in those people, things, and events for which we are grateful, we show up differently. We call in different energy and a greater potential. What if we chose to be grateful for and appreciate the learning we got when something didn't go as we expected? It helps us keep learning and expanding our container of possibility. And this openness to learning keeps us in a growth mindset.

Another practice you can do in gratitude is to picture a golden thread from your heart to the person for whom you are feeling gratitude, whether they're alive or not and whether you're grateful in joy or in learning. As you breathe in and out while reflecting on your appreciation, send that energy from you through the imaginary thread to their heart. Allow the giving and the receiving.

And last, people who choose to live in a gratitude mindset are frankly just a lot more enjoyable to be around. That kind of spaciousness helps our creativity and communication.

Key Questions

1. What are you grateful for today?
2. What do you appreciate about people or events that frustrate you?
3. What can you learn from those insights that you most appreciate?

Practice 6: Action
Committing to a Daily Practice

And now comes the call to action. Can you give yourself a handful of minutes each morning to breathe in these values, visions, intentions, and gratitudes quietly, committedly, and consistently for the next year? It starts with just your commitment to quietly breathing in a value you want to embody each day. Breathe it in and allow it to fill your being. Breathe the value out, allowing it to swirl around you, creating an expanding field of energy and allowing you to consciously spread that word or value out into the world. If your mind wanders, that's okay. Just gently ease it back to focus on your value.

After a few minutes of breathing, take a minute to write down your intention or intentions for the day. Based on that value, how do you want to walk into the world today? Please begin your intentions with "I am," allowing the mindset to come into the present with your intention. If you write in the future tense, such as "I will" or "I want to," your intention may also stay in the future, just out of reach. Visualize and feel the intention.

"I am effectively listening to the needs of myself and others."

"I am completing the project on my desk with joy and curiosity."

"I am engaging with my partner and children with love and patience."

Whatever comes to mind, commit those words to paper. Doing this work daily allows deepening and provides a space between your actions and reactions. This practice of awareness, intention, and gratitude allows you to bring to bear more powerful and thoughtful responses, expanding your creativity, potential, and conscious effectiveness.

Last, take a minute to write down something or someone for whom you are grateful today. As you write one or more examples of gratitude, don't just write them. Feel them. Breathe in your thankfulness. Take a breath to reflect on what you learned from the experience or the person. When we teach ourselves to live in a gratitude mindset, our world opens up. We see life's journey as one of learning and expansion. We become more open to our own curiosity. We become more vulnerable and less judgmental. We expand more into our own potential and veer away from becoming stuck in blame or victimhood.

And this is where the practice starts—first with awareness of our ability to choose how we show up; then with our own thoughtfulness and self-articulation about how we want to show up and what we want to bring to the world; then with small steps in the flow to align our roles and behaviors with those values, vision, and purpose. The practice is solidified by the daily action of taking a few minutes every day to breathe, set intentions, and be grateful. This is the work of reflecting and remembering. Let's begin.

What commitments of this practice do you want to make to yourself? How often? When during the day works best for you to reflect and journal? Be specific. Put an alarm or reminder in your calendar. It begins with just a few minutes a day—ground yourself, breathe in your values, set an intention, and send out a gratitude. Perhaps write your specific intentions each week about small steps in a certain role in your life that will help you bring in the core value by which you want to live, and then reflect on how it went. How did you feel? What began to shift? *Small steps; seismic change.*

5

The Practice

n the following pages, you'll find fifty-two short reflections or essays, originally written as blog entries, along with writing prompts for your intentions, gratitudes, and reflections. These essays are intended to help you think. They reflect my insights along my journey over the last year. Some essays may feel relevant, while others may not. The idea here is to help you get into the practice of coming back home to yourself each day before you go out into the world.

> "Whatever you think you can do or
> believe you can do, begin it.
> Action has magic, grace, and power in it."
> — Johann Wolfgang von Goethe

"Reflection is no longer a luxury but necessary for our survival."
— Dr. Dan Siegel, author and positive psychologist

Welcome to the Show

Week 1

One fall morning in 2009, my now ex-husband, Chris, woke up not feeling so well. *A flu bug?* we wondered. We thought that, worst-case scenario, it could be Lyme disease. We were getting ready for a big family adventure—a year in Jackson Hole with our five children. Life was about as bright as it could be. How could anything get in the way of our dreams?

Then, as a colleague of mine likes to say, "Welcome to the show." Lyme disease became advanced brain cancer, and well, everything changed. Everything, except for perhaps the most important thing: *How do we want to show up every day? What are the values that will hold us through the darkest of nights?*

It has been quite the journey since then of understanding that all this effort we put into the external definitions of success is rather hollow without a healthy internal center around *why*. And money, while important, can't be the primary answer. Because honestly, we can all probably live with a lot less and be just fine—and we can't take money with us when we die.

I've seen many examples lately of people running so fast that they don't have enough time for what we know to be good for our health, like nutritious food, exercise, and sleep, and ignore the whispers of their emotions while moving forward with the force of a steamroller. And when I ask why, the silent pause can be deafening. I get it, and sometimes I'm right there too.

I had an experience with Chris that I hope few have to go through. But many of you have and know you can wake up one day and find that everything is different.

Ambition is fine. Dreams are important—but without our health (physical and emotional), nothing really matters. Knowing how fragile life is and how scary it is to be on the verge of losing someone with whom you have built your life has taught me the power of clarifying our internal compass.

Ask yourself these questions:

1. What is most important?
2. What can I do to best be of service to myself, those I love, and my community?
3. What do I want to stand for and deepen into on this journey of life?

When we answer these questions and take a few minutes to reflect on them every day, our fears lessen. We become more courageous concerning what matters. We know why we make the choices we do.

Yes, I am an idealist and an optimist. But the medical data, employee loyalty and satisfaction data, and relationship data keep proving that taking a few minutes to slow our bodies down, breathe deeply into our values, set intentions, and come from a place of gratitude reveals a healthier, more connected, and more prosperous person.

And when "the show" comes to us, we can weather the storm without breaking our sails. Here's to inhaling love and exhaling fear on a daily basis.

Writing prompts above

"I Am" Statement

_____

_____

_____

"If you are not leaning, no one will ever let you down."
— Robert Anthony, organizational theorist and
professor of management control at Harvard

Leaning in to Leadership

Week 2

I first became interested in the power of leadership training in the late 1980s, when I went to a "Seven Habits of Highly Effective People" workshop at Procter & Gamble, where I worked. Stephen Covey's principles just made easy sense, and I could remember them.

The first principle in Seven Habits is "Be proactive, not reactive." In other words, take responsibility for your own attitudes, feelings, behaviors, and ideas. Don't lean back and wait for someone else to fix a problem or, even worse, just complain on the sidelines without directly trying to be a part of the solution. Listen deeply, be impeccable with your words, make clear agreements, and commit (kind of like Don Miguel Ruiz's advice in *The Four Agreements*).

I raise these ideas because I have been seeing interesting *aha* moments with leadership students and clients. We all have lots of ideas. We can learn all of the skills, models, and behaviors of effective leaders, but eventually it comes down to one question: "Do we want the change enough to lean in?"

Whether in a professional or personal situation, do we want to take the personal responsibility and initiative to work toward the potential we see in our minds? Are we willing to take the leap to get to the other side:

- To listen more deeply to ourselves and others?
- To become microscopically honest?
- To work through to clear alignment on agreements?
- To personally commit?

Leadership is about each of us breathing deeply, stepping in, and trusting that, as we walk forward with clarity and inner alignment, the bridge will appear.

That's why the work of understanding our deeper values and our vision for how we want to show up in the world is critical. Understanding our inner purpose, or as I like to say, our inner bull's-eye, is so powerful. It helps us remember who we are when we get into tough situations.

This awareness reduces our sense of risk because we know why we are making certain decisions and actions. This awareness also allows us to pause and take a breath before reacting. It brings us back home to ourselves before impulse, adrenaline, and fear can jump into the driver's seat.

If you feel any places in your life where there is some angst or frustration around an opportunity, pause. Think about what the leader inside you who aligns with your values would do and lean in. Expand into possibilities. Listen, be honest, clarify agreements, and observe any shifts. Taking a few minutes each evening to reflect on your observations in your journal can continue to deepen your growth in awareness.

Writing Prompts

1. What frustrates you?
2. How does that conflict with your values?
3. How can you grow by recognizing this?

"I Am" Statement

_____

_____

_____

"One step is all it takes to find your bridge—one "yes,"
one act of courage, one radical thought, one shift
in perception, one dare, one prayer, one moment of
forgiveness, one apology or one phone call...either you
can wait, or you can start walking."
— Robert Holden

A New Light on Leadership

Week 3

Years back, I had an incredible three-minute thrill: I watched a full solar eclipse through the point of totality. Until that moment, I was skeptical of how powerful seeing the moon fully covering the sun could be. It was an image, experience, and feeling that will always stay with me. And here's why—for the previous 20,444 days of my life, the sun had always shined its light, whether through clouds or blue sky. Yet, what I experienced on July 2 in La Serena, Chile, was the visceral realization that patterns can be changed, and quite inspiring effects are the result. Even if only for a few minutes, the long tail of the shift remains.

Here's how it impacted me with regard to leadership. Typically, we think of leadership as

- knowing who we are (the values and beliefs we aspire to live by),
- identifying where we want to go (our vision, purpose, and mission),
- clarifying how we are going to get there (our strategies, milestones, and action plans), and
- developing the skills to empower and inspire other resources and people to help us get there (our key performance indicators, communications, and meetings).

And then there's the deeper level of leadership, which leads to questions like these:

- How do we listen and stay open to learning from different perspectives?
- How do we grow from mistakes or challenges and not solidify in our judgments against ourselves or others?
- How do we learn to trust and be vulnerable and not try to control so tightly?
- How do we become aware of when we are operating from fear and constriction versus creativity and openness?
- How do we truly learn to forgive and release the weight of anger that we may feel fuels us but actually exhausts our systems?
- How do we stay compassionate and humble enough to say "I'm sorry," really mean it, and learn from it?

And that becomes the even harder work of leadership. Oprah Winfrey once said, "True forgiveness is when we can say, 'Thank you for the experience,'" and as I like to say, thank you for the learning. To me, that is the daily practice of deepening into the values we want to live by and consistently becoming aware of and releasing the reactive energy associated with anything that is different than our expectations.

We give it our best. We learn. And we grow in our ability to reflect on our judgments, to see fears as opportunities to understand our own projections and what we may want to work on within ourselves. As the saying goes, "The issue isn't the issue. It's how we deal with the issue—that's the issue."

The practice of Six Minutes Daily is designed to help us understand who we are and where we want to go and then to daily allow ourselves a few minutes to quietly breathe in light, reflect on our intentions and ways we can break old patterns, and end with focusing on something for which we are grateful. Having that practice made watching the eclipse more magical. No matter where we've been, today is a new day to build the small steps of change to create the people we truly want to be and the world in which we want to live.

Writing Prompts

1. What mistakes have you made in the past week?
2. How did that make you feel?
3. How can you grow from them?

"I Am" Statement

_____

_____

_____

"Feeling states, thoughts and images can actually cause chemicals to be released, enhancing the ability to grow T-cells."
— Jeanne Achterberg, author of *Imagery in Healing*

Allowing the Feelings

Week 4

I lived in Boston for seventeen years of my adult life. I think of those years as my creative power years. My family was creating babies, building careers and businesses, and designing homes that would be secure bases for our children. It was truly the full-on time of my life, and I am deeply grateful for the families and soul sisters who were navigating similar journeys and for all the connections and memories we share to this day.

Our family left Boston and moved to Jackson Hole in 2010, but one recent weekend I was back in Boston and able to spend some spacious time with these old friends. We are all in our midfifties now, and all the kids who pitter-pattered, giggled, and yelled down the familiar hallways and kitchens are now from seventeen to twenty-seven years old. The last of the high school graduations are nearly over.

So at every dinner, along every quiet walk, with every shared cup of coffee or wine, the question that echoed was the same: "What's next?" It didn't matter if they had stayed home or managed presidential campaigns, had birthed many children or chosen to be the world's greatest aunt or uncle, we all seemed to feel a similar mix of excitement, anxiety, grief, and twinkle.

The path of parental responsibilities and cultural expectations seems to have disappeared into a wide-open field of possibilities, sometimes feeling more like a scary minefield. There is no longer an endless list of to-dos for others and responsibilities to divert our attention when we ask each other, "What do you want for yourself?" There lies the wide-open possibility of time and choice.

As a woman, I believe there is also another piece to this shift that brings up strong emotions every time I allow myself to think about this newfound independence, and that is the visceral shift in touch. For so many years, we were burped and farted on; clutched, sometimes with death grips, especially if we needed to be somewhere quickly; grabbed around the legs; hugged tightly around our necks; held a growing hand in ours; snuggled at night; and of course, told how wrong we were by teenagers. Sometimes we escaped to the bathroom just to have a few minutes alone. That powerful, tangible manifestation of love and security fed us, even if it exhausted us at times. The absence of being so needed can leave a hole.

I think our opportunity here is not to fill the hole too quickly. The hole has painful moments, lonely moments, and scary moments—and it sometimes begs to be filled too quickly with a glass of wine, a *yes* before realizing we'd rather stay home and read a book, a bitterness around things that didn't turn out how we had wished, and even just the realization that the chance to make some choices has passed. (I guess it's time to face the fact that I may be too old to go to medical school).

But what if we allow ourselves some time to observe that hollow place inside? What if we give ourselves the space to feel all the emotions that arise from the emptiness of that void without judgment? What if we allow ourselves a few minutes or more every day to just send love to that hollow space—not answers, just love? Instead of finding a distraction for our loneliness, what if we breathe in the power of all that love we gave over the past few decades and really give it back to ourselves? And, with each breath out, we share the love we are cultivating for ourselves with everything around us.

During this reflective time of graduation, I want to honor parents in their second act of life and deeply thank my wise friends who so fill my heart with love as I write this.

May we allow this time of contemplation—and it takes time. May we know that the answers will come from our hearts first, not our heads. By being love, answers will come. We just need to allow

Sandy Schultz

ourselves to get quiet enough to listen and commit to the daily practice of cultivating a few minutes every day of that quiet breathing.

Writing Prompts

1. Write about something or someone who disappointed you.
2. Are you able to see why you felt disappointed?
3. Are you able to forgive yourself for feeling that way?

"I Am" Statement

"Someone is sitting in the shade today
because someone planted a tree a long time ago."
— Warren Buffett

The Key to the Golden Door

Week 5

A while back, I had the joyful and insightful experience of taking my eighty-nine-year-old mother and her friend on a three-day trip through Yellowstone. There was lots of talking; driving; and oohing and aahing at animals, waterfalls, vistas, and geysers. It was a magical three days of togetherness with two women from an older generation, without the normal distractions of life.

As we talked, my mom's friend shared that, as she grew up, no one ever asked her what she wanted in life. She got the message that the goal was safety and security. Now in her eighties with children and grandchildren, she laughed about how she learned the hard way that there was no golden door leading to security. She originally thought that once someone married the right person, had the right job, and raised the right children, all would be golden, but she soon realized it didn't always work that way. She now says that creating joy, peace, and success is her daily practice, and she is finding the golden door within.

The Golden Door Is Just as Murky for the Young

In another conversation, my oldest son told me that, last year, he thought he had his life set—he had a great girlfriend with whom he was looking for a house and work projects that were positively on fire. But a year later, the girlfriend was no longer in the picture (no house was bought), and business had its normal ups and downs. It was a challenging and powerful year for him. His goal of "being set" evaporated into the journey of life.

So often, we think that if we just get *there*, all will be fine—wherever there is. But then we realize that life is ever changing. What if there is no golden door except that within ourselves and the way in which we choose to show up?

You Have to Show Up to Realize Your Dreams

It doesn't mean we can't have fabulous, audacious dreams and goals. Dreams and goals motivate us and bring out our best work and creativity. Yet, if the view of achieving that goal is that a golden door will open and we will live happily ever after, we may want to recheck our thinking.

What if every day we set the intention to walk through our own golden door of how we want to show up in the world? We breathe in the love, trust, cooperation, synergy, creativity, and honesty we want to have in the world. We set an intention to discover, see, feel, and remember all the ways the world is helping us get there. We write down those reflections at the end of the day.

Step by step, we unfold into our highest, strongest, most courageous selves, knowing the golden door of joy and success is within us. I look at powerful women like my mom in much later chapters of their lives, having lived through many, many moments of sorrow and joy. They carry their own light, and nothing can take that light away. It makes me proud to be my mama's daughter, and maybe I'm starting to understand where some of my life's passions began.

And as I start to see my son recognizing this in his twenties, I am hopeful for the generation to come.

Writing Prompts

1. What brings you joy?
2. What sustains your joy?
3. How can you find joy within?

"I Am" Statement

_____

_____

_____

> "Just as the acorn contains a mighty oak,
> the self has everything it needs to fulfill its destiny.
> When the inner conditions are right, it naturally emerges."
> — Derek Rydall, screenwriter, stuntman, and author

Acorns and Oak Trees

Week 6

James Hillman, a Jungian psychologist and renowned author, first opened my eyes to the glory of the acorn in his book *The Soul's Code*. Think about it for a minute: every acorn has the energetic potential within it to become an amazing, unique oak tree. If you haven't seen the Angel Oak Tree outside Charleston, SC, it's worth a visit. It too began as an acorn, as we all metaphorically do.

Lately, I've been leading a visualization in which I ask clients to put their feet on the ground, close their eyes, shake their shoulders and necks, and take a few slow, deep breaths. I ask them to visualize breathing out any old stale air and any stuck ideas or grumpies and then visualize breathing in fresh, exhilarating light coming in through the top of their heads and flooding their bodies, awakening every cell with new energy and possibility. Try it.

Now, visualize the fire from deep in the center of the earth flowing up through the ground to your feet, allowing the earth to become your powerful foundation. See your personal acorn growing deep roots around values and principles of how you want to show up in the world and what you want to bring to the world.

As that foundation of clarity grows ever stronger, see the light from the sky filling you and fueling you to reach new horizons, allowing you to gracefully flow and dance in all sorts of weather. You are free but not lost. You are connected but not stagnant.

You know who you are, and you are ever growing. We can grow to our full potential without pushing. We can grow from within without adrenaline filled activity to the point of exhaustion. And we can become far more than we ever thought possible.

Try this visualization and then write down reflections. Ask yourself, *What is success?* Water that amazing acorn that lives within you and allow it to grow.

Writing Prompts

1. How are you watering the acorn within you?
2. What do you want to grow into?
3. What will you do to nurture yourself today?

"I Am" Statement

_____

_____

_____

"Love and work are the cornerstones of our humanness."
— Sigmund Freud

Remembering Our Humanness

Week 7

In August 2019, the CEO Roundtable (a group of top CEOs chaired by JP Morgan CEO Jamie Dimon) issued a statement saying that a corporation's responsibility was no longer just to uphold shareholder interests. Corporations must also invest in their employees, protect the environment, and deal fairly and ethically with their suppliers. Now, one could easily argue that doing those things actually benefits shareholders' long-term interest, but let's not argue semantics. Let's instead be the everyday leaders who do pause in our choices and check in with our humanness.

Balancing a need to be profitable with a need to support the health of our employees, the earth, and everyone we work with—as well as the health of those using or consuming our products and services—seems like common sense, right? It's kind of like how eating fresh fruits and vegetables, getting outside and taking a walk, and connecting with others directly (technology doesn't count) while earning a living also seem like wise actions to take. So why do these common-sense things often seem so at odds with how we live today?

Is it because we allowed it to happen; somehow, through the great power of consumer marketing and Freudian psychology, we allowed money and stuff to become the great behemoths defining success. How did everything else, including time, rest, healthy food, play, creativity, and connection become secondary? When did competition so powerfully overrule collaboration? If you Google "wealth inequality in the US," you can read many different perspectives on the shifts and trends in the last one hundred years.

Given the challenges to our mental, emotional, and physical

health as a society, I believe that the balance that the CEO Roundtable advocated is paramount to creating a sustainable, regenerative, thriving world.

These questions are not about politics. They are about leadership. Each of us carries profound leadership in our lives. The world is created through what we choose to value. And nothing has to come down to *either, or.* It can be *yes, and.*

The Century of Self, a documentary on Edward Bernays (Freud's nephew who's often credited as the father of modern advertising), highlights some of the earliest steps that helped get us to this cultural place where material and financial gain often override our deeper knowledge about health and prosperity.

I am excited that corporate leaders have opened the door to valuing balance beyond Wall Street profitability. I hope they continue to think about balance when it comes to health, connection, and prosperity. As leaders of our own lives, we can set an example by making daily choices to remember our humanness and think about why we are here.

Writing Prompts

1. Why do you think you are here?
2. What are your gifts?
3. How are you sharing them with the world?

"I Am" Statement

_____

_____

_____

"Always make time for things that make you feel happy to be alive."
— Anonymous

Marvelous Night for a Moondance

Week 8

Earlier this month, we were treated to the October hunter's moon. I was in my own busy world, oblivious to it, until it snuck up on me while driving to a meeting. Through some magic, I was in the right place at the right time to witness the moon rising. I stopped, pulled over, and snapped this picture.

I stood in awe of that moment. How could anything be so beautiful? And then I wondered, *How many moments do I whiz past without witnessing the power and energy of what's around me, without giving thanks to this spectacular planet and the power of nature within it?* Yes, I live in Jackson Hole, a place where it's hard to deny moments like these when you see natural beauty in wide open spaces. I've also lived in Chicago, Detroit, Cincinnati, and Boston. There are spectacular places to connect with nature everywhere.

Nature holds the power of wonder—whether in the simplicity of a butterfly or the rage of a storm. And there is a growing body of reliable data showing that nature holds the power to heal us. Nature, itself, is medicine. A walk through a stand of trees or along a pond impacts our human systems in a positive way. Nature slows us down; it awakens new neural pathways to creativity; and it brings in new oxygen to reenergize us.

And at a time when nature most needs us to realize her power and potential, we are migrating indoors to our technology at an alarming rate. In doing this, we are missing out on the awe of moments like the moonrise. We are missing out on all of the healing power nature can provide.

Experience a Moment Outside and Tell Us About it

So here's my challenge to you: sometime in the next week, can you find some time to go outside, look around, and let nature in—and if possible, share that moment with someone else? See what it feels like to slow down and let the trees or the water or the fields surround you. And then, do it again and again, frequently. As nature in our northern hemisphere gets ready to rest and rebuild during the darker winter months, feel her pulse and connect to her wisdom. And reinforce to others, especially our children, that if we don't honor nature, so much of what makes us healthy humans will be lost.

Writing Prompts

1. How does nature make you feel?
2. What do you notice when you are still in nature?
3. Where do you find that feeling close to your home?

"I Am" Statement

_____

_____

_____

"Time is a created thing. To say, 'I don't have time,' is like
saying, 'I don't want to.'"
— Lao Tzu

Love Doesn't Tell Time

Week 9

What a journey it's been since I wrote my first Six Minutes Daily blog! It feels like I've been to more graduations, reunions, weddings, life-changing events of the older generation, and friend-focused adventures than ever before. You probably have too. It has been a time of intense reflection, family challenges, and business ups and downs. I find myself sometimes having an out-of-body experience, like an observer in a kaleidoscope of connections with people I have known and loved for twenty, thirty, forty, and even fifty-plus years.

And here's the crazy thing—while activities, to-do lists, and accomplishments fill our days, love knows nothing of time. When we reconnect with old friends and family, a decade could feel like a day, and years collapse together such that laughing about events forty years ago makes them feel like they happened yesterday.

That is the power of love and human relationships. Frustrations and differences seem to melt away with bonds of connection. What was so challenging and important once may not hold as much energy now. Questions become much more focused on "How are you?" rather than "What are you doing?"

Perhaps this is why I am so powerfully drawn to this mission of asking you to take six minutes every day to remember who you are and how you want to show up before you run into the busyness of your life. I am not diminishing accomplishments or achieving goals. They are important motivators toward progress and growth.

I am simply asking you to spend six minutes each day looking inward before you run out into the world. Reflecting on where you are going and why, along with what is most important, may help you remember to breathe before you react and listen before you respond.

In this small way, our actions and activities can become powerful extensions of the values we want to embody in our jobs and our relationships and in how we treat ourselves. It is our beautiful gift to ourselves and a great practice to pass on to our children.

We do get to choose how we show up every day and how we prioritize our health, and the health of the relationships around us. It is in the multitude of these small steps that we can light up our world and find the courage to keep going even when obstacles arise. Love knows nothing of time.

Writing Prompts

1. How do you feel when you reconnect with old friends?
2. How do you want to show up for them?
3. How do you want them to remember you?

"I Am" Statement

_____

_____

_____

> "It is the power of memory that gives
> rise to the power of imagination."
> — Akira Kurosawa, Japanese film director

Memories and Thanks

Week 10

Forty-plus years ago, at age sixteen, I took my first trip to Europe to visit my aunt, uncle, and cousin. My Detroit-born aunt and uncle had gone to Paris on a bicycle trip in the early sixties and—well, they never returned to live in the States. A few years after I was born, they too, had an only daughter. Although an ocean apart, Vivian and I developed a close relationship.

Over the last decade, we have been busy raising children and dealing with lives, so we've only seen each other once. This week of Thanksgiving wonderfully changed that track record. Instead of celebrating a beloved Thanksgiving in Wyoming with children and friends as we usually do, my youngest son and I flew to Europe to celebrate with our broader family. And boy, did my French godson grow tall while maintaining his joyful smile.

After a special weekend of family and homecooked French meals, my son and I walked the many steps of Mont-Saint-Michel and ate oysters next to the seawall in Cancale, Brittany—things I had done with my family on that first trip forty years earlier.

It was a remarkable feeling to see how my memory matched with reality (very closely). As we dipped our oysters in butter and drank a glass of wine, I told my son that, if someone had given me a book as I was sitting at dinner in the same place back in 1979 and said "Read about your life," I would have turned the pages gasping in awe—both at the beautiful and the painful moments.

I stared out at the sea, as I would have avidly read the book, feeling such gratitude for every part of my life: for the wonder that forty years had passed in an instant and for the realization that I'm still standing and able to share these memories with the next generation.

So I wanted to share an idea as we bow our heads at this time of Thanksgiving. Go visit a place that was special to you as a kid and that you haven't been to since. Maybe it was a camp or the first tree you climbed. Go there and allow the space to wrap around you. Reflect on the child you were, full of ideas and hopes. Now, look across the road of your life. It wasn't always easy. Chances are there were some pretty hard moments. Yet you are still here, so you made it and so did I!

We've learned. We've loved, and yes, we've lost. Such is life's journey. May we find much to be grateful for as we breathe through the years. May we also think forward to the next decades in wonder and wisdom. With luck, the stones upon which we are standing will still be here, waiting to help us remember all that life gives us and all that awaits.

Writing Prompts

1. Where were you when you were ten, eleven, or twelve?
2. What do those memories conjure up?
3. Can you be grateful for those moments?

"I Am" Statement

_____

_____

_____

> "Values are like fingerprints. Nobody's are the same,
> but you leave 'em all over everything you do."
> — Elvis Presley

No Matter What the Weather

Week 11

Recently, Jackson Hole got its first glimpse of winter—cold rain and snow in the mountains and some freezing temperatures at night. And then, summer returned, with daytime temperatures in the midseventies.

It reminded me of how much we can't control in our lives. All we know is that change comes, whether it's the weather, relationships, jobs, or the fact that children quickly become adults.

The question "How can I show up as who I want to be no matter what the weather is around me?" is challenging. Transitions can be tough because hopes, expectations, and dreams are hard to realize. We are human, and that means that we have emotions.

So how can we allow our beautiful humanness to shine through the cold rain and early snow? One way that helps me is the practice of creating and consistently breathing in value-based and behavior-based intentions.

My Ground Rules for Creating Intentions

1. Make them simple.
2. Begin with "I am."
3. Be positive, not negative (it's about what we want, not about what we don't want).
4. Be inspiring and empowering.
5. Use an active voice by adding "ing" to your verbs.
6. Make sure they aren't half hearted. Instead of trying or hoping, focus on being and doing.

What's the Point of Creating Intentions?

Intentions are an inspiring, action-oriented, and simple way to fire you up to become who you want to be. Some intentions are big muscle memory shifts, and some are simple, daily ways to practice bringing forth bigger things in our day.

Here's an example, my big intention this year: "I am thoughtfully slowing down and consciously choosing when to say yes." Anyone who knows me is probably laughing. Remember, it's about the daily practice and evolving personal clarity and awareness.

I set daily intentions that relate to what is planned over the next twenty-four hours. As an example, "I am allowing space between my meetings in order to show up fully prepared." Intentions are personally honest, vulnerable, and deeply aligned with the meta values of who you want to be. And they evolve. Truly, it's just a few minutes a day of you focusing on yourself.

Instead of saying, "I will try to feel like I belong here," "I will do my best to listen," or "I will not get frustrated too easily," an effective intention is actually being in the state you want to be. "I am discovering and joyfully seeing all of the ways I belong here," "I am deeply listening to the exciting ideas of my team," and "I am living joyfully and compassionately no matter what the weather."

Intentions are about helping us stay in our own power of choice versus becoming a victim of life's circumstances. The idea of an intention is to really allow our bodies to feel the success we want to embody.

Try It

This week, pick a value you'd like to embody. Write a simple, positive, action-oriented intention. Write it on a sticky note and put it on your bathroom mirror. Take a minute to breathe in that value every morning or evening. Then before you go to sleep, take a minute to write down ways that you brought that intention to life.

Writing Prompts

1. Pick a value that you want to show up as, come rain or shine.
2. Ask yourself, *Was I (patient, kind, loving, etc.) today?*
3. Write down a success story.

"I Am" Statement

_____

_____

_____

"In the happiest of childhood memories,
our parents were happy too."
— Robert Brault, American author

A Page from My Mom's Journal, October 26, 1956

Week 12

I walked down the basement stairs of my childhood home to start the laundry, as my mom or I had done for the past fifty years. As the wash got started, sentimental sounds came forth—my footsteps clanking on the stairs, the water rinsing through a hose that once jumped out of the sink and onto the floor. (I think, somehow, I had been responsible for that mishap—oops.)

I walked around the small, cement basement, seeing the shadows of my friends and me playing dress-up or grocery store in one corner and watching my mom teach me how to iron in another. I thumbed through dusty boxes that included some of my first record albums— the Beatles *Blue* and *Red* albums and Queen's *A Night at the Opera* (my first album ever).

On a small shelf laid some rather unkempt magazines, notebooks, and a dusty old copy of the *Better Homes and Garden Cookbook* my mom had used throughout the sixties and seventies. I opened one five-by-eight leather, three-ring binder filled with yellowing lined paper. The top of one page was dated October 26, 1956. The next line read "Educational Psychology," and notes were scribbled down the page. A reading list had been folded and tucked into another page, and a dog-eared tab marked a page with a bunch of sentences in Spanish with notes and vocabulary.

Mom's handwriting hadn't changed much in all of these years. It's funny to think of all the things that have happened in her sixty-six years of life since then, yet her handwriting remains the same. She was a student at Wayne State University in 1956, and she would soon marry my dad. A few years later, I was born. As I held her notebook, I felt such poignancy—the innocence, hope, and optimism of a college student with her life's journey ahead of her.

I felt deep love and pride to also see the tapestry of her life from that point on—the beauty and the heartbreaks, the good times and the very hard times she's endured.

Upstairs, at age eighty-nine, her body was showing signs of age, but my mom's inner strength, cheer, and spirit, like her handwriting, hadn't changed much.

As I go through the challenges of seeing my mom grow old, challenges that many of us are dealing with right now, I ask myself, *How do I stay grounded in love during both easy days and hard days?* We are human. We make mistakes. We get caught up with emotions and insecurities, and we make choices that sometimes hurt the ones we love the most. And sh-t happens. Unexpected surprises of all types and sizes wake us up.

Perhaps the key is to learn not to sidestep the pain or challenge while also not wallowing in it for too long, lest we get stuck in victimhood. At this darkest time of the year, when light will soon slowly return, may we all take the time to tap into that deeper source of strength and love within us.

The last line of David Whyte's poem "Self Portrait" says it so well: "I have been told, in that fierce embrace, even the gods speak of God."

May we all remember how loved we are and how worthy we are. Life is a journey; each step is an opportunity to grow and learn without judgment.

Writing Prompts

1. Can you conjure up the smells from a happy childhood memory?
2. Did your parents ever share a vivid childhood memory with you?
3. Did that make you feel loved?

"I Am" Statement

_____

_____

_____

> "The bad news is time flies;
> the good news is you're the pilot."
> — Michael Altshuler

Waking Up on Time: Reflections in the Mirror

Week 13

Earlier this week, I was having a conversation with a wise and respected friend who has participated in some of my workshops.

"Can I ask you something about Six Minutes Daily?" he said.

"Of course," I replied.

He looked at me directly. "Why are you doing this? You ask all of us developing entrepreneurs to answer that question, yet I haven't heard your answer. How committed to this work are you? Because it seems to me that it will take immense focus and really leaning in to make it go."

Gulp. When you see your reflection in the mirror, sometimes it can be both wonderful and painful. So I decided to write about it. This is why I'm writing this book and launching a mobile app with tools to support people.

It feels like I've woken up ten minutes behind for decades, always running to catch up and never getting there, no matter what I accomplished or achieved. And I've lived through the impact that mindset has had on relationships, health, and my overall world. What I've realized is that we are only enough when we feel enough inside, which can mean doing the internal work of acceptance, forgiveness, and compassion first for ourselves and then for others around us.

With the daily practice of internally believing in our value, we can wake up with space, consciously understanding that we have choices in how we show up and what we prioritize. Six Minutes Daily is, in some ways, a gift to my most beloved, adult children as they learn about navigating the world. I hope it is a reminder to them that success begins inside of us, before we ever go outside.

Regarding my commitment to this work, it is impossible to not follow your calling, even if there are bumps, bruises, and winding paths along the way. Now my work is to build in the time, structure, discipline, and flow to allow those goals to become real. In the quiet darkness of late fall, what is it that I commit to?

Writing Prompts

1. What do you want to commit to?
2. Why wait until next year?
3. What small step can you take now toward that goal?

"I Am" Statement

_____

_____

_____

> "We should always allow some time to elapse,
> for time discloses the truth."
> — Seneca

Smarter and Faster

Week 14

For almost forty years now, I have felt like I woke up ten minutes late each day. The to-do lists of kids, work, dogs, and life stuff started filling up before I even opened my eyes. If only I were smarter, faster, more organized, more efficient. Now, I realize I was starting my day from the wrong place.

When you read the words *smarter* and *faster,* how do they make you feel? Where does the energy of the words land in your body? Often when I ask clients or workshop participants this question, they say things like, "In my shoulders," "My chest got tight," "My head got tense," "My body crouched," and "I got ready to run."

Or they say, "Yes, that's what I need to do, and then I would be successful," or "I would be worthy." *Smarter and faster* seems to have become the mantra of our culture.

I'm not saying "smarter and faster" doesn't have a place in the world. It most certainly does. But waking up to that mantra every day is exhausting and counterproductive to achieving a thriving life and building a cohesive team, organization, or family.

Now breathe in the words *slower* and *better.* How do those words make you feel? Often, I hear things like, "I can breathe," "It helps me relax," "It sinks deeper into my being," and "It allows me to think of new possibilities."

Smarter and faster is a mental construct that can easily kick up our adrenaline. It tells us we need to move; we need to become more efficient. It reminds us that some predator is coming up on our heels. And often, that idea comes before we've asked these three questions:

1. Where am I running from or to?
2. Where does the path lead?
3. Is that where I want to go?

When we build from a basis of *slower and better* on a daily basis, we allow our minds and souls to pause. We allow ourselves to both ask and answer these questions.

Rarely do the answers come as some grand epiphany that changes everything. More likely, they provide subtle shifts.

1. What does it feel like to breathe in *slower and better* as you walk into a conversation?
2. Does it remind you to ask yourself, *How do I want to show up in the conversation?*
3. Does it allow you to ask yourself, *What is my desired outcome of this conversation?*
4. Does it help you think about the deeper desired outcome instead of just an immediate emotional reaction?
5. Does saying "slower and better" allow you space for creativity?
6. Does it create an internal pause long enough to think *What if?*

From a biological and physiological perspective, *slower and better* returns cellular energy to our vital organs (our hearts, brains, and livers) in our core. When we focus our energy inward instead of letting it travel on adrenaline highways to our arms and legs, doors open to new creativity, innovation, and possibility. We learn to think and see expansively. We understand connections we may not have seen before. We become more aware of the choices we make that can have major implications for our physical and emotional health.

I wish I would have learned this message decades ago, but better late than never. Try it. Slow down for a few minutes and just breathe in a new mantra—"slower and better." Write down what comes to your mind and allow yourself to be grateful, even for the smallest thing. Ask your team, family, or friends to do the same. Take a minute to slow down together before a meeting or a meal. Observe what happens if you allow more time to pause and think before you act.

"I Am" Statement

_____

_____

_____

"Happiness is when what you think, what you say, and
what you do are in harmony."
— Mahatma Gandhi

Efficiency Needs a Counterbalance

Week 15

A few weeks ago, I was having a conversation with my French cousin about the state of the world and our countries. I said that I believe part of the challenge in the culture of the United States is our seemingly ever-increasing obsession with efficiency without the counterbalance of long-term effectiveness.

She responded, "You know, in the French language, we only have one word—*efficacité*—that means both 'efficient' and 'effective.'" I was fascinated by this—that in French, one concept doesn't exist without the other.

When I think of French culture, I think of longer vacations; a focus on cuisine, dining, and conversation; and perhaps a slower pace of life. I'm not trying to romanticize the French as perfect, as they, too, have significant challenges. However, this word in their language makes me think that long-term effectiveness and shorter-term efficiency may be complementary. What does that do to decision making? This week alone, headlines showed that Boeing introduced shortcuts for efficiency with tragic results, and our government is promoting policies that ignore environmental impacts to speed up infrastructure projects.

What Does Long-Term Effectiveness Mean?

Our long-term effectiveness depends on our values. To prioritize effectiveness, we need to have some awareness, clarity, and alignment about how we want to be effective. *Effectiveness* is defined as accomplishing our purpose and creating our intended effect.

- What is our purpose?
- How important is our health?
- What about our planet's health?
- How important are our relationships?
- Is our ability to communicate also important?

Efficiency can narrow some of these answers to seem black or white. It is defined as accomplishing something with the least waste of time and effort. It is about speed. With speed, complexities can be left behind. There becomes very little grayscale. Variables become either good or bad. Stock prices often rise and fall based on short-term gains, not long-term strategy.

It's not that efficiency is bad, yet without thinking about our longer-term purpose or desired effect, there is no counterbalance. And we could easily end up in the wrong place.

Walmart and Amazon are the behemoths of efficiency. But what have they done to diversity on Main Street America? In a world obsessed with efficiency, we may end up with a few winners and a lot of losers.

Balancing Efficiency with Effectiveness Starts Within

Balance begins with asking ourselves these questions:

1. How am I leading my life?
2. How am I setting expectations for my family, team, or organizations?
3. What is my purpose?
4. What is the desired effect?
5. What values become my central foundation to success?

Then we can ask ourselves, *How do I most efficiently get there?*

Our choices count. Our voices count.

And so I come back to my mantra. Create a few minutes of space for reflection every day to ask yourself these questions. With small steps every day, we can courageously make our values and purposes central to our decisions and the way we show up in the world. It is about balance—step by step.

"I Am" Statement

_____

_____

_____

> "When you arise in the morning, think of
> what a precious privilege it is to be alive—
> to breathe, to think, to enjoy, to love."
> — Marcus Aurelius

Ancient Wisdom

Week 16

My son Jimmy was reading *Meditations* by Marcus Aurelius, a Roman emperor from the first century (yes, I had to look that up). I laughed when I realized that Aurelius's ideas from nearly two thousand years ago are still so true today and much of why we created Six Minutes Daily. Then, as I was writing this week's section, a student of mine sent me something that confirmed the same teaching.

I smiled and shed happy tears. Again, it's not like these thoughts are a secret. And it's one thing to read them or hear them and quite another to live the daily practice with a loud and busy world out there pulling us in many other directions.

One key for me is to commit to the daily practice of remembering who I want to be and how I want to live and holding onto something each day for which I am grateful, even on the toughest of days. It's not about perfection or, goodness knows, I would have failed long ago. It is about the journey of learning and growing and getting up when we make a mistake with learning and kindness to ourselves. It is about taking the time to know where our centers are so that our activities, behaviors, and actions begin to turn synergistically from a balanced source.

It's funny how some thoughts stay in our world for thousands of years after they were written.

Writing Prompts

1. What is a simple pleasure for you?

2. How do you express gratitude for your simple pleasures?
3. How can you share a compliment with someone who helps you enjoy those simple pleasures?

"I Am" Statement

_____

_____

_____

"Every champion was once a contender who refused to give up."
— Rocky Balboa

The Power of Will

Week 17

Will—kind of a funny word. As a verb, it has us leaning into the future, getting to all the things we hope to do. "I will …" with no expiration date. As a noun, it holds two meanings. One is a document stating how we want our resources to be distributed after we are gone. Another is the will to survive, to succeed—invoking an internal power that allows us to do something far greater than we thought possible.

If you haven't watched the original *Rocky* or seen the character's run in the two-minute YouTube video, it might be a great evening activity. Or perhaps watch the ninth inning of game seven during the 2003 pennant race between the Red Sox and the Yankees. Talk about *will*.

Will is the stuff of courage, heroism, and human spirit. Rudyard Kipling's lines from his poem "If" best summarize this:

> If you can force your heart and nerve and sinew
> To serve your turn long after they are gone,
> And so hold on when there is nothing in you
> Except the Will which says to them: 'Hold on!'

There's a lot of talk these days about grit, resilience, and perseverance, which are all powerful and necessary traits for staying in the game and achieving our dreams. But they are focused more on the finite container of our being.

Will includes that but somehow goes beyond. It's not grit or persistence that allows someone to lift a car off of someone else or cut off an arm to escape being trapped in a canyon. Will invokes a primal desire to live and to love.

When that deep, unconditional feeling gets included in the equation, the power within us grows beyond anything we could imagine as physically possible. Our egos and fears of failure and unworthiness fall back in the rearview mirror. They just don't matter so much anymore. The deeper connected love of the journey, of life, of others, and of our hopes and values supersedes our smaller selves. It's not so much about us anymore as it is about life and giving all we have to the moment.

We all have dreams that can easily get dashed by our fears. At least I sure do. But when I breathe in my will, something happens. Love brings its own courageous knight to help me overcome fear.

When I quietly breathe and check in with my deeper will, I get a better understanding of whether I really want whatever it is or not. Can I find that deeper well of energy, or is my idea, vision, hope or built just on adrenaline, which will soon run thin?

Will creates an interesting internal checkpoint. So take a few minutes this week to breathe in love to ask yourself about your deeper will. What insights come up?

Then go watch *Rocky*.

Writing Prompts

1. What are you willing to do this week?
2. What does your will say about this?
3. Does your will align with your values?

"I Am" Statement

_____

_____

_____

> "What makes the elephant charge his tusk in the
> misty mist or the dusty dusk? What makes the
> muskrat guard his musk? Courage."
> — The Cowardly Lion in *The Wizard of Oz*

Courage

Week 18

Courage is not the absence of fear. It's the ability to find inner strength to continue to go forward despite the fear. *Courage* is derived from the word *heart* (in Latin, *cor*). Its original meaning was "to speak one's mind by telling all one's heart."

What if we took the idea of courage one step further and thought of it as the ability to actually pull fear out of our limbs and into our cores and then push it, along with our negative thoughts, into our expansive hearts? From there, we could transform the power of fear into love—calming it with breath, holding it within, and allowing its energy to turn into strength and clarity.

These times call on us to find our courage. In an external world filled with so much uncertainty, the knowledge that no one can take away our inner foundation and determination to show up becomes even more powerful. We hold that choice.

The more we bring our fears back into our hearts, the more we can slow down our adrenaline and bring our energy back to where it is most needed, in our cores.

- Centered energy is creative, problem-solving energy.
- Centered energy is responsive, not reactionary.
- Centered energy allows us to gain strength and power.

Teach yourself a new habit. When fear arises, take thirty seconds to close your eyes and visualize energy flowing like a column of light into your heart while you breathe in love. You may have to do this many, many times per day, but it will change how you show up and how you rebuild for a brighter future.

I'm committed to rebuilding more structure in my life from the inside out. How? Exercise, connections (with physical distance but emotional closeness), and friendliness to all the neighbors we've passed by as strangers before. I am putting down my phone and looking into the eyes of my children, friends, parents, and partners and really just being with them. I am reading, playing games, writing, listening to music, and walking.

What would it feel like to make the personal plan you've long dreamed of if you had a little time to track your daily commitments? We can relearn where our source of energy comes from—within. The book *Leadership in Turbulent Times* is a powerful, inspiring read. It reinforces that we are resilient.

May we do our daily practice with courage, reenergizing through the power of our hearts and finding the strength and answers from our own centers.

Writing Prompts

1. What makes you feel courageous?
2. Why?
3. Can you remember a time when you responded to a challenge with poise and courage?

"I Am" Statement

_____

_____

_____

"Expose yourself to your deepest fear; after that,
fear has no power, and the fear of freedom shrinks
and vanishes. You are free."
— Jim Morrison

That One Nagging Thing

Week 19

Is there something that you've told yourself ten times you need to do? Is there a conversation, project, email, errand, bill to pay, or something else that lurks in your head like some sort of pendulum, swinging in and out of your thoughts, only to be pushed away and to swing back again?

I have had something on my to-do list for weeks, and I have been a ridiculous procrastinator. For me, it was finalizing the music and licensing agreement so the app for *Six Minutes Daily* could actually come to life and go into beta testing. It's a project that took less than an hour when I finally did it. But my mind has spent way more than an hour over the last few weeks finding ways not to do it.

When I asked my entrepreneurial students and coaching clients if they had one nagging thing to get done, everyone said yes. Why do we allow ourselves to get in these negative feedback cycles and drag our feet on things that we are called to do? One big answer is *fear*—fear of success, fear of failure, fear of conflict, fear of … the elusive ghost in the closet that is often so subconscious that we can't even articulate it.

This fear can drain us. It allows the voice inside to have a heyday, reminding us that we aren't good enough. But that's really just our insecure self-image or ego wanting us to stay small. We can shift that voice.

How? *Welcome the fear* (and the feeling). Instead of writing that thing on your to-do list again, knowing that you're not ready to do it, give yourself a few minutes to have a conversation with it. Mentally, put the task in a chair across from you. Ask it why it is being so hard to complete. *Let it respond.* Write down what comes. Respond back to it with your inner courage. Ask what it is trying to teach you. Use creativity to come up with new solutions to the fear. Keep welcoming the internal dialogue, and keep writing down the conversations. By facing our fears and allowing them to have a direct dialogue with us, we can learn from them, answer them, and help overcome them.

Usually, nothing is awful in reality as our imaginations make it out to be. I found that, especially this week, when I had a conversation with my fear around success, rejection, failure, and control, it lost its almost paralyzing power, and it became easy to move forward and finish my project. After I selected the music, I found my excitement again and my energy surged. I am here now, I am okay, and I am ready.

Here's to facing and talking to that one nagging thing on your list this week and releasing it so that you can move forward with energy and possibility.

A few minutes of breathing and writing down our intentions and our gratitude every day helps to awaken our inner knowing. Let's fly!

Writing Prompts

1. What is that one nagging thing that you can't seem to get done these days?
2. Ask that thing you can't get done what success means to it.
3. How does it feel to talk to fear?

"I Am" Statement

"Take a long pause ... breathe and know that things are
happening for you, not to you."
— Ashton Kutcher

Finding Grace with Space

Week 20

Between the moment something triggers us and our reaction, there
is space. Within that space, we have a choice, and when we make
that choice, our reality emerges. Even if that space is a split second,
there is time between the stimulus and the reaction to check in with
our values. We can ask, *Where do love, patience, responsibility, and
understanding fit in?* Or we can react without thought from our ancient
reptilian instincts around fear, safety, and ego protection. Our minds
work at lightning speed, so it is not a matter of having enough time.
Infinity can be found in a second. It is a matter of practice.

The exciting thing is that reality can be shifted every time we
make the next choice in that space, for there are infinite spaces in our
days. This is how consciousness can shift and how muscle memory
can go from reactionary to expansive.

Here's the catch, though: In that split second of space, we need
to take responsibility for our words and actions. Instead of staying in
wounded, victim consciousness or ego greatness, we need to open up
to our deeper power and let the light in, so to speak.

I have two recent examples. One was when some friends went
shopping for a dinner party and bought some expensive wine. Upon
opening the car door to get the groceries, the wine fell out, breaking
on the driveway. *Stimulus, space, response.* In that split second, the
energy of the evening could have gone several different ways that
could impact relationships and the future. Instead of anger, my friends
reacted with an amused laugh. One got a broom while the other went
back to the store and carefully held the wine all the way home. The

evening was full of joy and laughter, good learning, no blame, no guilt—just awareness and ease.

In another example, a family was getting ready for school and work, but when the mom went to grab the keys from their usual hook, they weren't there. Immediately she said to her husband, "What did you do with the keys?" He quickly responded, "I didn't take your f-cking keys," and a significant blow-up ensued. No one used the space between stimulus and response to their benefit, and the entire household's relationships and stress levels were impacted.

It is easy to blame and much harder to take responsibility for our own actions. But we do have the ability to change the course of our reality and future by taking that responsibility. Step by step, see if you can find some grace within the space.

Writing Prompts

1. Can you remember a time when you reacted poorly?
2. Can you remember a time when you reacted with love, patience, responsibility, and understanding?
3. What was the outcome of each?

"I Am" Statement

_____

_____

_____

"We have roots that grow toward each other
underground. And when all the pretty blossoms have
fallen from our branches,
we find that we are one tree, not two."
— Louis de Bernières, English novelist

What If...?

Week 21

What if underneath all the things we do every day, the words we say, the clothes we wear, the challenges we face, the pains we carry, and the choices we make, there really exists a deeper self? And what if that deeper self doesn't have a color, a status, a race, a religion, a resume, a bank account, or even a story?

What if that deep place inside *all* of us is made of only *love*—infinite, all-encompassing, awe-inspiring, simple, yet vastly profound love that carries no judgment and no criticism? It is a love that simply doesn't care about the details.

And what if we allowed that kind of love to fill us, wrap around us, and support us in releasing ourselves from self-judgment and in being able to forgive, really forgive, ourselves and others? What if that love that is in our deepest selves was connected to the love that exists and resides within every other living thing, like the roots of a vast, interconnected tree universe?

And what if, in this kind of love, there is no past to hold onto and no future to aspire to? There is only living in this present moment, filled with love.

Just think about it. What if, between now and the end of the year, we allowed ourselves to bathe in that kind of love, even just for a few minutes every day? What if we allowed ourselves to let go of the helping, the doing, the leading, the fixing, and the searching, and we just let the love in?

1. From that place, what is one thing you would do differently today?
2. What is one way you would see love in the faces all around you?
3. What is one way you would be kinder to yourself today?

And if your mind quickly goes to something like, *Well, isn't that just an excuse to be lazy and indolent?* then ask yourself, *Is that love? Or is that my mind just trying to fight against the simplicity of the idea?*

Here's the crazy thing. When we look at the essence of all major religions and thousands of years of philosophy, it's kind of what they all said—that love, peace, virtue, and self-acceptance are the essence of life.

So join me in this. Give yourself a few minutes every day just to sit in the feeling of love and let every cell of your body be bathed with love from within your infinite well. It's pretty amazing to observe what this practice might do for your health and relationships too.

Writing prompts above

"I Am" Statement

_____

_____

_____

> "Grace is the voice that calls us to change
> and then gives us the power to pull it off."
> — Max Lucado

Grace in Stormy Weather

Week 22

For twenty-nine years now, I've been blessed to share Christmas morning with my children. What changes there have been from the giggles at six in the morning and toddlers running to the tree to the cozy, hugging wake-ups of today with coffee brewing at nine o'clock. This Christmas includes global smiles from Brazil, Turkmenistan, Uganda, Mexico, and the good ol' USA as my sons bring home their friends and loved ones.

As I sit here in solitude at the kitchen table, relishing the opportunity to cook in the quiet magic of our home (as everyone else went out skiing for a few hours), one word keeps coming to me—*grace*.

Earlier this morning, I had a conversation with my son's friend from Turkmenistan, a dictatorship, who's spending the holidays with us. She said that the people in that country learn to find happiness from family, loved ones, and good health as everything else around them is propaganda irrespective of truth. She said human rights and women's rights get drowned out, so joy is found close in.

That was profound to me. So what is the definition of grace? It involves 1) simple elegance, 2) courteous goodwill, 3) to do honor or credit to, and 4) spiritual strength and healing. Earlier this week, my friend Ariel Mann read me this philosophical definition of *grace*:

> How you climb up the mountain is just as important
> as how you climb down the mountain and so it is
> with life, which for many of us becomes one big,
> gigantic test followed by one big, gigantic lesson. In

the end, it all comes down to one word. Grace. It's how you accept winning and losing, good luck and bad luck, the darkness and the light.

I'm not trying to be a downer on Christmas. I feel the deepest of love and gratitude for family, friends, and health—for the life I have been given. And yet, I hold a weight of worry. I've always believed that we Americans could wonderfully challenge one another about ideas, policy, and law yet all have some common set of agreed-upon facts and information.

I sit thinking about grace because I don't know what to do when it seems that, these days, many people don't even care about the facts. I feel a bit like a boat in stormy seas without an anchor. My existential struggle stems from the fact that I teach holistic, authentic, values-based leadership with *love* as the foundational value. It's powerful. It works. And it gets hard when the leadership we see demonstrates a different kind of value.

So, as we go into this new year and new decade, I set my intention on all of the above: simple elegance, courteous goodwill, honoring those I believe in, and asking for strength along the journey and living in that strength, no matter the weather.

I will do my best to embody grace as I navigate the stormy sea of life, doing what I most believe in to bring joy, success, health, and healing to those around me. Perhaps if we all committed to grace— even for just a few minutes a day—some amazing things would happen.

Writing Prompts

1. How do you define *grace*?
2. Can you see grace in the dark as well as the light?
3. How will you commit to grace this week?

"I Am" Statement

_____

_____

_____

> "Resolve and thou art free."
> — Henry Wadsworth Longfellow

Be the Resolution

Week 23

Happy new year, new decade, new energy, new opportunities!

In these first few days of the new year, before the next Monday comes and the engine of daily life begins to fully roar, I have a thought.

Before jumping into resolutions, let's look backward and reflect on our journeys over the last ten years. Let's allow ourselves to breathe in the power and the courage it took to still be standing here now.

1. What challenges did you overcome that you can look back on with a new perspective?
2. What moments of joy would you like to reach into your memory bank to remember and relive how it made you feel?
3. What accomplishments and milestones are you most excited by or proud of and why?
4. What lessons did you learn that can guide you into the next decade?

There's one more layer to this reflection exercise. Let's break down all these questions to examine the various roles we play in life (roles like partner, parent, daughter, son, sibling, friend, professional, community member, spiritual member, healthy being or athlete, hobbyist).

When you reflect on these moments and examine your roles in them, what ideas come up? What shifts might you want to make? What areas do you want to focus on? How might you shift the balance of your time and priorities?

I don't mean to overplay the new year of 2020, but symbolism is powerful. Twenty-twenty is the mark of clear sight and vision. We hold the power within ourselves to grow, expand, learn, and manifest. Yet it doesn't happen if we don't choose to give our lives some conscious focus and awareness. From that awareness comes our commitment to small steps that deepen into our own powerful and thriving health, where connection and success arise.

Create a Resolution about Being, Not Doing

As we turn our focus to New Year's resolutions, here's another thing to consider. Let's not create resolutions that involve doing; let's create resolutions that are about being.

Let's make resolutions that

1. reinforce how we want to show up in the world,
2. deepen into the values we want to embody for our entire lives and the roles we play, and
3. help us remember how we want to create and expand rather than react, especially in challenging moments.

I suggest this because, if we focus on our being, the doing will naturally come. But if we focus on the doing without taking a look at our deeper frameworks of being (who we are, how we want to live, and how we want to show up), the commitment to doing can quickly lose momentum. We just get stuck in old patterns.

Exercise

Here's a simple but profound exercise to begin our "being" resolutions.

1. Go to the list of values in this book.
2. Write down the ten values that identify how you want to be and how you want to be thought of no matter what role you're in. These values do not have to be fully true right now—they can be aspirational.

3. Now look at your list and cut out five values, leaving you with the five values you most want to bring forth in your life—perhaps they're the concepts and thoughts you would most like to hear from others as they celebrate you on your ninetieth birthday.
4. Get two sticky notes and write the top three to four values on each of them.
5. Put one sticky note on your bathroom mirror and one on your computer or car dashboard.

Reflect on those words every day for the next month, and set an intention each morning on how you can bring these values to life that day in one of the roles that you play. Observe what evolves. Perhaps take a few minutes every day to write down your intention and later write down any reflections on how you felt when bringing that value to life.

*   What did you learn?
*   What might you want to do tomorrow?

By giving our attention to our being, quiet shifts begin to occur that lead to seismic changes in our relationships, health, professional effectiveness, and success. We are the change we seek.

Writing prompts above

"I Am" Statement

_____

_____

_____

"Integrity is doing the right thing,
even when no one is looking."
— C. S. Lewis

Digging Deep and Leaning In

Week 24

My oldest son, Brolin, is from Uganda and had dreams of going to the 2018 Olympics as the first African freestyle snowboarder. Often, we create visions like this and work toward them, but the demons of self-doubt linger (I know this feeling all too well). We find ourselves asking, *Am I worthy enough, good enough, deserving enough?*

Cyclical questions like these are hard to overcome. How can we allow our fears and the defensive protection of our egos to release enough that we can dig deep and fully lean in? How can we breathe in that failure only puts us back to where we are right now—and think of all the learning we'll have had along the way?

In 2017, that's where Brolin was—working out a plan and dealing with the mental (and sometimes physical) speed checks before going off a jump. Those speed checks come in all forms: procrastination, anxiety, and unconscious self-sabotage. And sometimes *fate* intervenes with a health issue, an accident, or a financial crisis, saying, *If you truly want this, you're going to have to dig deeper and prove it.*

As parents, my ex-husband and I used to tell our sons, "Character is what you do when no one else is looking." Fate is the related wake-up call, asking, *Are you ready to believe irrespective of all of the pressures from the external world?"*

Brolin's fateful moment came in Kazakhstan at a top world snowboarding event in 2017. His heart had some strange hiccups, putting him in the hospital and pulling him out of the needed competitions to get enough points for the 2018 Olympics.

It would have been easy to throw in the towel, but he dug deeper and created a daily practice to let go of many of those internal demons. Over the last two years, while also gaining his master's degree in public health, he has diligently practiced (mentally and physically) and practiced and practiced.

His health is better than ever, and more importantly, his mental speed checks have dramatically diminished. He is leaning into his dream with the power, courage, and knowledge that, whatever happens, he will always give it his best shot. COVID and the resulting cancellation of so many qualifying events made it very difficult for athletes to gain enough points to qualify for the 2022 Olympics. However, Brolin continues to ride with his team as an Olympic hopeful. This is one of the many stories behind Six Minutes Daily. It helps remind us every day to breathe in our courage and breathe out our fears. As we become more conscious of our internal drivers, we can undo old patterns and help those fears disappear—or at least go on vacation to Tahiti for a very long time.

Can you take a few minutes today to allow yourself to breathe in deeply, relax, and give every cell new oxygen? Breathe in the value that helps you smile and connects to your deepest knowing and courage. Consciously breathe out and release old fears that don't serve you. Then take a couple of minutes to write down your intentions for the day—reminders to yourself that a powerful, deeper you is waiting to help. And please, stay in a growth mindset by thinking through and giving thanks to something or someone who helped you along the way.

To learn more about Brolin's story and to help him make his Olympic dreams to represent Africa in the Winter Olympics, check out the feature film *Far from Home*.

Writing Prompts

1. What is your dream vacation?
2. When are you going?
3. How can you overcome your fears and lean in to make it happen?

"I Am" Statement

_____

_____

_____

"Live your own life by a compass, not a clock."
— Unknown

Seeing into Brave Spaces

Week 25

This week, I've had the honor of working with leaders in Puerto Rico to define and deepen into their purpose and open up vulnerability. We are beginning to see how their vulnerability can help them further strengthen their teams and organizations. It is truly astounding to see what happens when people allow themselves to be more fully seen and give their full attention to seeing one another. Synergistic magic emerges as we remember our humanness and expand into the potential that comes from stepping into our authenticity.

A colleague passed on the poem below. It captures the power of creating brave spaces for one another. As you walk through your week, see what happens if you spend a few minutes every day seeing someone fully and holding a brave space to listen, learn, and connect.

Love grows deep roots in brave spaces.

An Invitation to Brave Space
by Mickey Jones

Together we will create brave space
Because there is no such thing as a "safe space"
We exist in the real world
We all carry scars, and we have all caused wounds.
In this space
We seek to turn down the volume of the outside world,
We amplify voices that fight to be heard elsewhere,
We call each other to more truth and love

We have the right to start somewhere and continue
to grow.
We have the responsibility to examine what we think
we know.
We will not be perfect.
This space will not be perfect.
It will not always be what we wish it to be
But
It will be our brave space together,
and
We will work on it side by side

Writing Prompts

1. How have you been vulnerable at work or in your relationships?
2. How did that resolve a conflict?
3. How can you be vulnerable this week?

"I Am" Statement

_____

_____

_____

Good to Great

Week 26

A few days ago, one of my leadership students sent me a picture of her getting her nails painted by her eleven-year-old daughter with a text saying, "Thank you for reminding us that leadership is about paying attention to the moments and how we want to show up."

It was a sweet picture and reflection. All week it's had me thinking about how easy it is to run through the days, checking off our to-do list while potentially not leaning into the moments that matter most.

When we talk about effective listening, it is always heartwarming, inspiring, and a bit concerning, albeit humorous, to hear the stories that people bring back, such as, "Wow, I had the best conversation with my partner, colleague, child, friend." I often ask, "Isn't it interesting that you talk about a back-and-forth conversation when the exercise was about listening?" Their takeaway is that listening reminds them of the power of connection in meaningful conversations. The power of being present can change everything.

When we truly give ourselves to the moment (the moment Ram Dass coined "Be Here Now"), we consciously prioritize being right where we are. Research shows that words account for only about 30 percent of what we take away from conversations. Where does the rest of our learning come from? Connection, body language, eye contact, and so on.

All of this thinking brings me back to some of the key questions in effective leadership:

1. How do we want to show up in the various roles we play?
2. How do we define success in our roles as a professional, parent, partner, sibling, and so on?
3. What are the values that we want to embody holistically and authentically?

When we take a few moments each day to ground ourselves in that awareness and set intentions, our inner voices can remind us to remain authentic throughout the day. Our listening deepens. Our awareness of what is important deepens. And that deepening allows us to lean into our highest priorities and begin to release activities, projects, behaviors, and relationships that keep us running but don't deeply serve our vision of what's important and who we want to be.

That deeper listening, both internally and externally, can truly take us from good to great.

Writing prompts above

"I Am" Statement

_____

_____

_____

> "The most significant transformation for me has been learning (and relearning) that most of my valuable contributions happen when I'm in my purpose."
> — Brené Brown

Good Humans vs. Successful People

Week 27

Earlier this week in a yoga class, my instructor suggested that we put our primary focus on being good humans versus on being successful people. When we consciously prioritize and choose the actions of being good humans, success follows in all its forms (connection, abundance, thriving health, etc.). Yet when we prioritize being successful people, which too often in our society gets defined in external, financial, and material ways, the benefits quickly run thin.

This framework of the good human versus successful person has stayed with me all week. A few days later, I was in a conversation with two of the top realtors in Jackson Hole as they discussed the concept of collaboration and teamwork in what has typically been a very competitive industry. They reinforced that decisions that focus on honesty, collaboration, and integrity win if you want to build a sustainable, long-term business—and their results show it.

The people who run the clothing manufacturer Patagonia live by their values more deeply than most other companies, and again, external success continues to follow. When we do good, good things follow—in abundance, leadership, wellness, and connection.

The internal work for each of us comes from answering these three questions:

1. What does it mean to be a good human?
2. What values do I want to live by?

3. What gifts can I bring to the world? How do I want to be remembered?

It is the daily practice of connecting to those questions and allowing the awareness and answers to emerge that can bring about a profound shift in how we walk in the world. The shift comes in the quiet, small steps and choices we make every day. It is the pause before action that reminds us about our connection to our definition of being a good human.

It's like creating our own internal six-pack abs for how we want to live. Six packs and a strong core come with daily exercise and disciplined eating habits. Some days, we feel great about the practice, and some days, not so much, but we keep practicing. It is the same with clarifying our values and living by them—from our hearts, not just from our heads.

Honesty to self and others, integrity, reliability, compassion, connection, responsibility, doing our best, courage, kindness, resilience, authenticity, grit, and most of all, love to self and others are some of the values often used to define being a good human. So pick a value. Take a few minutes every morning this week to breathe it in. Then write down an intention around it along with words of gratitude for someone or something or just an internal lesson in service to our humanness. Observe what happens. Together we can create a thriving, sustainable world inside and out—and success will follow naturally.

Writing Prompts

1. What are three core values that define who you are?
2. How have you displayed those values this week?
3. Have you been successful without those values?

Sandy Schultz

"I Am" Statement

_____

_____

_____

"Yesterday is gone. Tomorrow has not yet come.
We have only today. Let us begin."
— Mother Teresa

Trust and Presence

Week 28

One year ago, I began writing blogs and posting them as Thursday Thoughts. I can't even really say why. Something just compelled me. Some weeks were easy, while others were not so much. But I kept showing up to this computer and trusting that my thoughts and insights may be of some benefit to someone.

The challenges of a global pandemic have woken me up to why I was compelled to begin—for those four little people, now adults, in the picture above (as well as Brolin, Miguel, and all the other amazing young people I have had the joy of seeing grow up over these last two and a half decades). They deserve my best and our best.

I've also gained clarity around what I'm trying to say, holistically, in my work. Yes, Six Minutes Daily is about the quiet shift and seismic change, but to what? I believe it is to support us in the awareness that we hold the power of choice in how we show up in all the places we show up. And those choices make the difference in the outcomes of our lives. That is how I define personal leadership.

Yes, we are in very turbulent waters. And we have all navigated turbulent waters before, even if not exactly like this. What did we learn that worked? For me, having dealt with a fair amount of death and loss at an early age, three main lessons come to mind.

Time for Trust

Take time to trust, believe in, and create a vision for a brighter, better future. See it, breathe it in, and allow yourself to feel it. Even if only for a second, hold onto that energy because together we can create it. Don't spend much time at all in blame or victimhood. That choice doesn't serve a brighter future.

Time for Presence

Be present now, right now. Be honest. Be vulnerable. Be real. Look into people's eyes. Shine your love and your light with the realness of your humanness. Right now. Breathe in the fact that the birds have begun singing louder than ever and that the sun still rises every day in the east.

Time for Resilience

We have two parts to our brains—the creative, visionary right side and the analytical, detail-oriented, be-here-now left side. If we want to be resilient, we need to use all the tools in our toolboxes to create flow between present and future and between trust and presence. Resilience is about keeping our feet on the ground and walking forward, even if we shake.

Writing Prompts

1. What does trust mean to you?
2. Write about a time when someone you trust was present for you.
3. Think of a time when you were resilient. Write about how that felt.

"I Am" Statement

_____

_____

_____

> "To see a World in a Grain of Sand and a Heaven in a
> Wild Flower, Hold Infinity in the palm of your hand
> And Eternity in an hour."
> — William Blake

Reawakening Wonder

Week 29

On April 10, 2019, my daughter and I spent eighteen dollars to get fifteen two-day-old chicks. Thirteen survived, and four months later, we held our first egg. It was a very exciting moment.

Anyone who knows me well has heard me fantasize about having a farm. These days, though, checking for eggs and growing a small garden are as far as I've gotten. The commitment of a farmer to spend hours every day working in the dirt would be a major shift and is still under thoughtful consideration.

But first I'll explain why I love chickens and gardens and dream of a farm—and why it's relevant to our work at Six Minutes Daily. These activities, whether for an adult or child, are daily touches of wonder. Wonder is that sense of awe, that breath that takes us out of life's daily routine. They stop us, if even just for a second, to remind us there is more. Maybe for you, wonder comes in the funny thing a child says, in the unexpected kindness of a stranger holding the door open for you, or in the rainbows that follow rainstorms.

Wonder can wake us up. It can deepen our understanding of the connectedness of all things. It can help us slow down enough to consider other possibilities. That awe of realizing that a seemingly simple seed with some water, soil, and sunlight can a few months later produce huge pumpkins, zucchini, and tomatoes can help all of us realize what is possible when we expand our decision making. What if we considered the principle of creating the world we want for the next generation?

Today, this week, this year, observe what comes when you set the intention of seeing and feeling wonder in your work, relationships, and activities. What does it bring up in your thinking? What creative ideas come? How can you cultivate more wonder for others? How does wonder begin to shift our world?

Slow down for a few minutes. Relax and take a few deep breaths. Focus on the lifelong values you want to embody. Become aware of when the illusion of fear is

driving behaviors and decisions versus the deeper power of all that you are. Allow the fear to release. Breathe in courage and creativity. Cultivate wonder. Set today's intentions. Give gratitude for all the learning.

And, if you get a chance, watch *The Biggest Little Farm*. It is a joyful documentary.

Writing Prompts

1. What seed would you like to plant?
2. When do you expect it will germinate?
3. How do you think that will feel?

"I Am" Statement

_____

_____

_____

> "Our mothers always remain the strangest,
> craziest people we've ever met."
> — Marguerite Duras

For the Love of Mom, Breathe

Week 30

A few days ago, I got a call from my dear mom, Irene, who's eighty-nine and still lives in my childhood home in Livonia, MI. Her greeting went something like this: "Hi, Sandy. I just wanted to tell you that I love your blogs…. And I had one little question: are you breathing in what you're writing?"

Inhale. Pause. Exhale. We both burst out laughing.

"I knew you were going to ask that," I said. "We teach what we most need and want to learn."

You see, all my life, my mom has been the voice inside my head asking why I run around so much. Twenty years ago, she even wrote up a contract about slowing down and asked me to sign it.

I share this for two reasons. First, I want to reinforce that these blogs first began as journal writings to myself. I've studied and am practicing what I write—and it is a lifelong journey with stumbles, falls, and awakenings. Step by step, we all choose how we walk forward. For me, taking internal time, becoming more conscious of how I want to live, and aligning what deeply matters to me (my *why*, so to speak) are bringing about profoundly positive shifts in my life. I am also seeing these shifts in the students and clients with whom I work.

The second reason I am writing about my mom is because of the way I reacted to her words. I love my mom deeply—don't get me wrong. Yet, over the decades, we've had our emotional challenges. I think a lot of our difficulty stems from my taking her words in a fear-based way, which only makes me angry and brings up every internal demon I have carried around about my own worth.

When my mom brings up questions about my busyness, I interpret them to mean that I am not good enough. I hear the questions as criticism and think, *I can never do it right.* I get frustrated, sad, and angry—the lowest and heaviest of emotions. As humans, we can get stuck in the mud with those emotions. We exhaust ourselves with their weight.

Thanks to the teachings of David Hawkins and Steve Chandler, I am learning about the "ladder of energy" and asking myself, *What would my reaction to or feeling about something look like if I consciously breathed in my emotions to climb the ladder, stepping up from fear and anger into creativity, potential, and love?*

This visual has helped me breathe and begin to shift. When I feel the triggers (the tightening of my being, the shortening of my breath, the unrest in my stomach), I close my eyes and breathe in deeply. I literally envision my body getting out of the murkiness of the mud and moving into the light. Maybe it sounds crazy, but it really works. In moving from fear to creativity, I start to see myself with different eyes.

With regard to my dear mom and her loving comments (that I've always internalized as critical), I am learning to relax. I smile. I really do breathe into love and gain gratitude for all she is and all she's given to me.

So during this week that includes Mother's Day, may we all take a few minutes to breathe up from fear, anger, and worry into expansive creativity. Love is an amazing thing—and we are all love. We each have a mother, whether here or somewhere else, who is doing the best she can. If we breathe in, relax, and set the intention to expand, perhaps we can be grateful for the lessons our mothers have taught and continue to teach us. I love you, Mom!

Writing Prompts

1. How are you challenged by your mother?
2. What do you love about your mom?

3. How can you thank her today?

"*I Am*" Statement

_____

_____

_____

"Scared is what you're feeling. Brave is what you're doing."
— J. K. Rowling

The Courage of the Young

Week 31

For the last week, I've had the joy of my cousins' visiting, including their curious and adventurous four-year-old son. As I played with him and observed his actions, I was reminded of a question: What would we do if the idea of failure didn't exist? What if frustrations, mistakes, and boundaries were only considered as learning for the next moment, day, week, or life?

I've been reflecting and journaling on this idea as it relates to my life, as well as talking to clients about it. There's often an expansive door of possibility opening when we let questions land inside. What would I do or say in my profession, relationships, and activities if failure wasn't an option and I was the only one responsible for my joy?

First, I want to mention that partying all night or traveling for the rest of your life may immediately come to mind, but I think those would quickly lose their luster as they may be distractions from what is really calling from deep inside. If we do a quick check-in with the values we want to embody in life and be remembered by, escapism is probably not on that list.

As I write down answers to the question, "What would I do if failure didn't exist?" I realize that the gap between my answers and how I currently show up in the external world is the degree to which "dis-ease" may be occurring. Dis-ease comes in all sorts of varieties—overindulgence (of food, alcohol, shopping, anything), illness, accidents, addictions. The gap can also show us the degree to which we're minimizing our own potential. The smaller the gap, the more internal alignment, synergy, creativity, power and energy flows in all we do. This growth mindset allows us to continually stay open to learning in our ever-increasingly fast-paced world. And that mindset takes deep trust and belief within ourselves—trust that we are enough and it's okay to be vulnerable. And it's scary to lean in like that because that voice of fear and failure is never far behind.

So here's my promise to myself for the next month, and maybe you would like to join me in this promise: Each day, I will pick a role that I play (professional, parent, child, friend, athlete, etc.) and write down the thoughts and answers to these prompts:

1. What would I do or say if failure didn't exist?
2. Then, set the intention and commit to one small step to lessen the gap between that answer and how I externally show up.
3. Finally, give thanks for my ability to dream.

Honesty, clarity, stronger boundaries, and less fear have all been a part of my emerging energy as I do this practice. What value emerges for you?

Here's to the wisdom of learning from a four-year-old.

Writing prompts above

"I Am" Statement

_____

_____

_____

"Nature does not hurry, yet everything is accomplished."
— Lao Tzu

Running Away from Happiness

Week 32

I sit drinking my coffee, watching a beautiful snowstorm this morning, and thinking about why I'm motivated to write these blogs.

Here's what comes. These days we all seem to have cluttered garages, closets, and calendars, irrespective of how much money we have in our bank accounts. It feels like our cultural drive to do more, have more, and be more is almost manic. *More* has become a key principle in proving our worth yet is a dead end for happiness.

I think of it as a speedway along which we all seem to be revving our engines to gain more, hoping to get somewhere—perhaps to a place where Bob Barker rings a bell, opens a golden door, and yells, "You won!"

But here's the thing—that door at the end of the speedway doesn't exist. No matter how much achievement, accomplishment, or material acquisition fills our lives, it still doesn't seem to be enough to find the elusive peace and joy we are seeking. And across many reliable and valid studies, research shows that, beyond getting basic food and shelter needs met, there is *no* correlation between wealth and happiness.

Our society is facing skyrocketing levels of depression, anxiety, stress-related illnesses, obesity, and addiction. I doubt anyone reading this book has not been touched by someone struggling with these challenges.

So what if there's another way? What if there's a way to take back our health, joy, peace, and success? What if, instead of just going down that horizontal speedway, we first breathed in a vertical line of energy around the human values we most want to embody for ourselves, our family and friends, and our world? What if we took a moment or two every day to slow down, lower our eyes, and breathe in values like kindness, patience, honesty, integrity, responsibility, compassion, and connection? And—dare I say it?—what if we just took a few minutes to deeply breathe in love (of self, of others, of earth, of any greater energy or God)? And then, what if we took a minute to breathe in something or someone for whom we are grateful?

Here's what research shows: when we begin doing this work around breathing up this vertical path of values, something begins to happen. We relax. We see things differently. We may actually see more success on the horizontal speedway of life, but we care less. We gain back our own power and our ability to make healthy choices. We improve our health as we feel the connection to the love around and within us. And we begin to realize that we have the power to change our future and our world. When organizations live by values first, financials and efficiency second, they win—and they win big. Look up the stories of Patagonia, Costco, Chobani, Tom's Shoes, Airbnb, Southwest Airlines, and Deloitte.

This isn't just touchy, feely stuff. It's quiet work. It's small steps, and it's incremental. But over time, this work of breathing in our deeper human values before we begin each day has seismic changes.

Writing Prompts

1. Do you remember a time when you put your values first?
2. What happened?
3. How did that make you feel?

"I Am" Statement

_____

_____

_____

"You have brains in your head. You have feet in your
shoes. You can steer yourself in any direction you choose.
You are on your way. And you know what you know. And
you are the one who'll decide where to go."
— Dr. Seuss

Yes, Our Health Matters

Week 33

Several years ago, I had the tremendous joy of seeing my oldest son graduate with his master's in public health from Westminster College. The dean said something in his commencement remarks that has stayed with me. He said, "We ask all incoming students, collaborators, donors, and faculty one question when they begin our program: Does your health matter to you?"

While we all typically respond to that question with a resounding *yes,* the data around our behavior tells a very different story.

What a question—"Does your health matter to you?" Of course, it does. We all know that, without our health, everything else gets compromised. Without our health, lives and dreams can dramatically change.

And, of course, a few days after the commencement, I got knocked down by a cold with a high fever. Go figure.

Health is typically thought of in three ways: physical, emotional, and mental. The human body contains twelve systems that all interrelate and depend on one another for effective functioning: circulatory, respiratory, digestive, excretory, nervous, endocrine, immune, lymphatic, integumentary, skeletal, muscular, and reproductive. Our human bodies are complex and awe inspiring.

Over the years, I've asked many doctors, "Why do some people get sick and not others?" whether we're discussing colds, the flu, depression, or cancer. The answer has been very consistent. It is some unknown and evolving formula related to genetics, environment, and behavior.

So if our health matters to us, do we seek information about our hereditary predispositions? Are we vigilant about preventing our exposure to chemicals and toxins in our environment? Are we doing our best to take care of our bodies?

Taking care of ourselves is a daily struggle, made up of decades of patterns, conditioning, personalities, and learning. How do we deal with stress? How do we relax? How do we deal with anger? What do we choose to put in our bodies? How do we translate our values into our behaviors?

When we run around, we don't take time to breathe and breathe deeply. When our bodies stay in an ongoing state of alertness against a perceived assault, our systems get tired. I am a living example of these words, as I sit in bed with a killer sore throat.

What if we didn't need to hold so much inside? How does it feel to breathe in understanding—to really forgive ourselves and others, to let go of judgment and replace it with learning on the journey? How does it feel to spend a few minutes every day breathing in our own healing, allowing the light of each beautiful day to fill our being? How does it feel to learn to listen before answering so that we can deepen into the knowledge that we are enough?

Data continues to show that these small steps dramatically help in our fight against disease and our ability to achieve long-term, radiant health. Please join me this week in spending a few minutes every morning to close your eyes and breathe in and out the word *health* or *healing*. Allow your body to relax into that feeling (I just did it and it really helped). Next, take a minute or two to write down an intention—just one—to do something this week in honor of your health, such as a longer walk, one less cookie, or a deep-listening conversation with a loved one or colleague, and then take a minute to write down something you're grateful for. Here's to our radiant health and the internal power of our amazing bodies.

Writing Prompts

1. What makes you feel healthy?
2. What can you do to repeat that pattern?
3. Does your health matter to you?

"I Am" Statement

_____

_____

_____

> "The fears we don't face become our limits."
> — Robin Sharma, author

Healing Begins with Breath

Week 34

Several years ago, the father of my children, thus one of the most important people in my life, went in for his third brain biopsy. He continues fighting a courageous and powerful battle against brain cancer even today. He has been given a reprieve. Sadly, invisible forces seem to have been working to allow in unwanted cells and transform them against the power of chemo.

Thirty-seven years ago, when I was in my twenties, my sons' ages now, I lost my dearly beloved father to the demon of alcoholism. Like a bad horror film, those memories of his last few months (my last few months of college) have started playing over and over in my head.

The spring of 1985 deeply impacted me because the world and structure I knew and the love I counted on went haywire. I didn't know what or whom to hold onto. So I began running. I began overfilling the moments of every day. And while I'm grateful for the many good things that have happened, I see now how they occurred not because of my busyness but perhaps in spite of it.

We can't outrun death. We can't outrun pain, sadness, anger, judgment, or grief. These feelings quietly rest on our backs, going right along for the ride whether we are running or ruminating. The faster we run, fill our plates, or try to distract ourselves, the tighter they hang on.

Here's what I am learning: healing begins when we slow down and then turn and face those difficult emotions. We can observe them and ask them what they are trying to tell us. We are so much stronger than our fragile egos or self-images might have us believe. Our hearts are powerful. When we slow down, consciously breathe, and observe our feelings, we also begin to build internal trust that we are enough, and we open up to forgiveness of ourselves and forgiveness of others for whatever wasn't as we wished. We become more whole. We begin to heal.

My daily conscious commitment to slowing down, mindfully breathing, and asking my deeper self for honesty and support makes me feel like I'm not gripping as much and not tensing my defenses against a perceived assault. I'm literally breathing myself up the ladder of energy, out of the constrictions of fear and sadness, and up to the expansiveness of love and creativity. I visualize myself breathing up this energetic ladder not just for me but also for my five children and, most of all, for their father as he goes into surgery.

We all have fears. We all care about someone who may be going through a challenging time. Today, take a few minutes to breathe in love and breathe out fear. Feel and observe your shift, your slowing down, your expanded awareness, and the new possibilities that come with this. Take a minute to write down any reflections and another moment to write down something or someone to whom you're grateful.

There are two commonly held acronyms for *fear*: Forget Everything and Run or Face Everything and Rise. It is your choice.

Writing Prompts

1. What are you afraid of?
2. How does it feel to say it out loud or write it down?
3. How can you share this feeling with someone you love?

"I Am" Statement

_____

_____

_____

> "The man who moves a mountain
> begins by carrying away small stones."
> — Confucius

A Two-Degree Shift Is Much Bigger Than You Think

Week 35

Here's a fun Six Minute Daily activity to open up doors to greater leadership, abundance, joy, and success. Stand up. Yes, stand up. Take a deep breath and move your shoulders back. Now pretend like you're standing on a snowboard with your feet about eighteen inches apart and bend your knees until you are in a squat.

Close your eyes and really feel your balance and the weight of your body on top of your feet. Now gently focus on moving your weight just one or two degrees more onto one foot (say, your left foot). Put 10 percent more weight onto that foot and imagine you are looking downhill. Become aware of how that feels in your body. Visualize pointing your snowboard down the mountain, leaning onto that weighted leg. Notice how the weight shift changed almost everything else in your body, from your ankles to your knees, your core, your shoulders, and your head.

If you had been snowboarding with your weight held differently for a long time, it might feel really uncomfortable. But as you practice it, it allows everything else to flow more gracefully. It gives you better balance and control, and it allows you to take on more challenging and difficult terrain. Although your whole being may want to lean back up the mountain, *the only way to improve is to lean forward and head down the fall line of the mountain.* (The fall line is the path a snowball takes if you throw it downhill.)

The same is true in our own growing awareness of our leadership ability. When we take just thirty seconds to breathe before we focus on listening to someone or starting a conversation, if we give ourselves a minute to think through what our desired outcome might be before we react to any situation, we begin to feel how just the slightest movement, pause, and breath allow us to *remember the values we want to embody or the longer-term goal, vision, or deeper purpose we have.* We quietly learn to create and act, not just react with old patterns and muscle memory.

This work can feel uncomfortable and bring up fears. The key is to begin small, to shift that one to two degrees and practice and practice again. The doors of your own ability to shift into your deepest leadership, success, joy, and abundance begin to open up.

Wishing you a great day from the mountains.

Writing Prompts

1. What does a two-degree shift mean to you?
2. How can you use that shift to embody trust?
3. Do you trust yourself more now?

"I Am" Statement

_____

_____

_____

> "Love is the Flower. You have to give it time to grow."
> — John Lennon

Being Bold about Love

Week 36

One day as my daughter and I were driving to Denver for my youngest son's college graduation, a friend called and asked, "What niggling blog bounces in your head that you haven't written yet?" It's funny how quickly I responded: "The one about love." I almost heard him smile. "Then write it," he said.

When we arrived, I asked my nearly adult children, "What would it be like if we all taught ourselves to breathe in love every time we walked into the next thing in our day—before every meeting, before each conversation or decision we made, as we got into our cars, as we stood in line at the grocery store, and on and on? How might that change our perspectives, our days, our lives?"

"That all depends on how we define love" was the consensus.

Often, we think of love as passive and just being nice. Somehow, we may think of it as swallowing our emotions and skipping to a smile. But we quickly realize that that isn't what love is.

My children and I all started to see and deeply feel that, while love definitely includes compassion and thoughtfulness, it also embodies honesty, clarity, creativity, authenticity, expansiveness, and responsibility. It means being kind enough to define and clarify agreements.

Then we all decided to try it. We thought about a challenging situation in our lives and consciously focused on breathing love into that situation. In discussing what had shifted, the words *ease, empathy, understanding, confidence,* and *patience* came up.

My youngest son realized that some of what he was doing to be nice and loving was really not allowing the other person to grow. Over time, he said he could see how that kind of love could lead to angst and easily fall into fear, anger, guilt, and other reactive emotions.

It's like the funny and real interactions of a group trying to decide which movie to see. If everyone becomes afraid to be honest for fear of hurting someone else's feelings, the group can end up going to see a movie nobody wants to see. Little growth or creativity comes. Energy shuts down.

Again, what if we breathe in *love* (of self, our friends, the day, the situation) before we start a conversation? How does that shift our perspectives, our priorities, our awareness, and our authenticity? And the even more interesting thing is that this could also be the definition of conscious and effective leadership.

My agreement with my children, as we began to celebrate the graduation weekend, balancing time among many different interest groups and activities, was that we would try breathing in love and see how it felt. It's truly a heart thing, not a head thing, to overanalyze. Will you join us? Slow down for five seconds before you walk into the next event in your day.

Writing Prompts

1. How do you feel when you give yourself a moment to breathe in love before shifting gears?
2. How did the next meeting, conversation, or activity go?
3. How did your body feel after that?

"I Am" Statement

_____

_____

_____

> "Of all the liars in the world,
> sometimes the worst are our own fears."
> — Rudyard Kipling

Remember, You Have Unlimited Potential

Week 37

I think of myself as a climber, albeit a very amateur climber. You know the kind—if it's at all steep or with any exposure, I want to be tied to a rope with lots of anchors in the rock in case I slip. And even then, my hands sweat.

Earlier this week, a friend sent me a video of villagers who live in the high cliffs of northern China. I watched in awe as people of all ages scampered along twenty-six hundred feet of rock face going down to town and up to their village, carrying everything from children to washing machines. These weren't *Free Solo* superheroes, like Alex Honnold. They were just villagers going about their day.

It reinforced for me all of the beliefs, boundaries, and barriers we often carry that block our potential. It reminded me of how stressed I can get about things that are so insignificant while missing the bigger opportunity of going for what quietly waits in front of me.

Ask yourself these questions:

1. Why do I think I need so many security blankets to feel safe?
2. Could some of these concerns be in my imagination?
3. What would it feel like to shift our paradigm and see there is a much wider view of what is possible?

What would we do? How would we lead? What new beliefs might we embody? I'm right next to you doing the same work. Or maybe it's not work. It's about letting go of some misbeliefs we hold.

It is the daily practice of breathing in our values, believing, walking into new intentions for ourselves, and being grateful for the journey that can open a new door to the future—and then, of course, walking forward.

Writing prompts above

"I Am" Statement

_____

_____

_____

> "Keep only those things that speak to your heart."
> — Marie Kondo

Tidying Up Your Life

Week 38

This morning, I reached for my little French press and small coffee grinder from my cabinet shelf, as is my morning ritual. First as I pulled them out and later when I put them back, I was highly aware of the small space into which they were squished. I looked at the shelf and realized that most of what was there, with the exception of my coffee setup, fills a lot of space, yet rarely gets used.

Then I looked at my pantry and saw the same thing, followed by my closet and my garage. Yes, I've read Marie Kondo's *The Life-Changing Magic of Tidying Up*, and I once spent hours deciding which sweaters magnified good energy for me and which I could give away. It is really powerful to declutter and lean into those things that bring us joy and not let them be lost among all the other stuff that we feel like we might want or need someday. And I see this takes ongoing practice.

Narrow Your Target Audience

As I then went on with my day, which involved teaching an entrepreneurial workshop, I had this thought: One of the hardest ideas for entrepreneurs to internalize is that our chances of success for a new business are many times greater if we start with a clear, easily delineated, narrow customer group. Yes, maybe our new bubble gum could be loved by everyone, but not really. There will be super users within the masses, and those are the ones we need to find, develop relationships with, and thank. Those are the people, like my little coffee pot, who deserve far more kindness, space, and focus than all the other stuff that gathers dust around them.

And then my brain began asking even deeper questions, like, *Why do I allow the people, things, and activities I love most to get squished in between all the other events, activities, and to-dos that aren't nearly as dear or important to me? How can I do the same decluttering of my daily to-do list as I do for my closet when there is a change of season? How can I better make space for what's most important?*

Ask Yourself What You Want

And then another voice inside said, *So what is most important?* And I realized that what is most important, besides my family, is my love for this country and the virtues and principles of integrity and character in which I grew up believing. In the fall of 2019, my dear friend Julie and I began this Six Minutes Daily journey in Las Vegas, where we canvassed for women who flipped the ticket in Nevada. Maybe you will join us in the future.

What an interesting thread of thoughts came from this morning coffee ritual.

Writing Prompts

1. What do you want to declutter from work or life?
2. What shines in front of you, patiently waiting for your attention?
3. What's most important to you?

"I Am" Statement

_____

_____

_____

"And forget not that the earth delights to feel your bare feet
and the winds long to play with your hair."
— Khalil Gibran

Grounding into Spring

Week 39

For the first time in six months, we here in the mountains are basking in temperatures above sixty degrees. The sun elicited a collective breath of joy and gratitude. I put away my down jacket and dusted off my T-shirts and shorts. I walked barefoot in the grass and lay down in a field, looking up at the blue sky.

Despite all the uncertainty and fear from our COVID-19 spring, I allowed myself to melt into nature—into the sounds, the smells, and the feel of the soft breeze and the pulse of the earth. These moments were a magical elixir, shifting the patterns in my brain and body to a place of peace and refueling me with new energy to go back into my day.

I encourage you to try this practice known as "earthing" as our unexpected spring opens up to May flowers. Touch the earth with your bare skin and pause for a minute. Close your eyes. Allow spring's magic to fill your senses. Let the earth hold you and all you carry for a moment or two. Put down your cloaks and your internal armor. Feel the pulses of this deeper knowing. Breathe. Allow the creativity and expansiveness to grow. There is no downside and lots of upside. Feel the ever-expanding light each morning.

Researchers say naturally occurring electrons in the earth ground our bodies by neutralizing damaging free radicals, which can cause inflammation and lead to disease. There is evidence that earthing improves our moods, blood flow, and heart rate; helps reduce stress;

and regulates our sleep. And there's even an Earthing Institute. Who knew?

Our physical, mental, and emotional self-care grows ever more important, and data continues to reinforce this innate power of nature to help us heal. (Check out Shiftjh.org for research-based data.) Slowly, our doors will begin to reopen following this pandemic.

As we mourn those who passed during the pandemic and hold those who are so very tired and scared, let us also remember the wisdom we gained from this time. What have we learned? How can we grow stronger, brighter, more vibrant, and more loving?

Yesterday, my dear friend who was my boss at Harvard Kennedy School sent me the poem below by Kathleen O'Meara.

Something Lovely

And people stayed home
and read books and listened
and rested and exercised
and made art and played
and learned new ways of being
and were still
and listened more deeply
someone meditated
someone prayed
someone danced
someone met their own shadow
and people started thinking differently—
And people healed ...
And in the absence of people who lived in ignorant
ways
dangerous, mindless, and heartless ...

The earth began to heal—
And when the danger ended
and people found themselves ...
They grieved for the dead
and they made new choices
and dreamed of new visions
and created new ways to live
and heal the earth fully
just as they had been healed.

Writing Prompts

1. What insights did you have when you sheltered in place during COVID-19?
2. How did nature nurture you?
3. How does it feel when you go outside barefoot?

"I Am" Statement

_____

_____

_____

"If you want to change the world, start off by making your bed."
— Admiral William McRaven

Commitment to Presence

Week 40

The other day my mom asked, "Do you still make your bed every day?"

"Yes," I replied.

She laughed and said, "It's pretty amazing. You've always made your bed. Me too."

We talked about how important this two-minute ritual is to give us structure, focus, and clarity at the beginning of our days. It creates closure to the past night and opens up space for a new day. It helps ground us in the present and creates order and a sense of control, especially when it's night again.

If you haven't seen this viral video, Admiral William McRaven says it best.

Last week, I mused on the helpfulness of grounding into the earth as a way to renew our energy and realign our jittery nervous systems. This week, I've been thinking about other ways to further help us regain our sense of presence, clarity, and alignment as the world outside continues to spiral in challenging ways.

Experts estimate that, on average, we are only about 20 percent mentally present in each moment. Our energy is all over the place—in the past and future but not in the now, not in this moment. When we focus on bringing our energy back to our selves, our critical thinking, creative abilities, and decision-making capacity improves. So beyond making your bed, here's a quick exercise to reclaim your focus and power.

Close your eyes. As you breathe in, ask yourself to pull your energy back into your core, back into your heart and your mind. Try this exercise a few times a day for a minute or two. Straighten your spine, close your eyes, and just concentrate on breathing your energy back into yourself. What does it feel like? What shifts inside? What new insights come?

Whether it's making my bed or breathing back in my overstretched energy, these practices strengthen my inner trust in the idea that *how I show up* becomes more important than *what is happening around me*. These habits deepen my sense of presence and widen my vision around choices regarding how to carry on.

What activities give you the daily consistency, clarity and structure to build your flywheel of energy?

Here's to our daily rituals and increasing our sense of presence.

Writing Prompts

1. What rituals do you enjoy?
2. How do your rituals make you feel present?
3. How can you share that presence with others?

"I Am" Statement

_____

_____

_____

"There is a world of difference between
searching for happiness and following your joy."
— Robert Holden

Expanding the Definition of Success

Week 41

How do you define success? I've been thinking about that idea all week.

Last weekend, I went backpacking with three lifelong friends who come to the Tetons each year for a few days of fun, friendship, and mountain climbing, even if our hair is turning gray.

This year, we chose an enigmatic peak called Mt. Thor, the eighth highest peak in the Tetons. We quickly realized that this adventure defined back country and bushwhacking in a way we'd never known before. On the second day, still more than fifteen hundred feet from the summit, we threw in the towel.

Our muscles were sore, we had scratches all over our bodies, and all of our food for the night was back at the edge of Leigh Lake. We failed to make the summit.

It was a hard call. We all are driven to achieve our goals. We'd spent time and money to get there, but we had overestimated our ability to move quickly through thick brush and boulders.

While we failed to meet our goal, we realized that success is not so linear, even though we often hold it as such. Here's where we succeeded—we laughed a lot and deepened our connection; no one got hurt; and we grew in our ability to boulder, bushwhack, cross rivers, and improve our fitness. We saw more wildlife than we'd ever seen in our previous five years of adventures combined. And we learned how to better prepare so we can have another go at Mt. Thor next year.

As I think about the deeper question of why we go on these

adventures, I realize that growing, learning, and loving are equally as important as achieving the final result. Perhaps, in some ways, those reasons are even more important.

How often do I—perhaps even we—focus so much on the goal that all the other values and deeper successes get overlooked, hurting our long-term health, relationships, and opportunity for greater prosperity?

As Dr. Seuss says in his wonderful book *Oh, the Places You'll Go,* "Life is a great balancing act." The more we lean into the deeper values of why we do something and how we want to show up, the more we may accomplish. The less weight we put on accomplishments and the more weight we put on how we want to show up in the world, the more we may become who we want to be.

It all begins with taking a few minutes every day to breathe in the values we want to embody, recognize the deeper successes, and set intentions to take small steps to lean into that feeling.

Writing Prompts

1. What is your ultimate journey?
2. How would you feel if you ran out of fuel to get there?
3. How do you define success?

"I Am" Statement

_____

_____

_____

"Feelings are like waves; we can't stop them from coming
but we can decide which ones to surf."
— Jonatan Mårtensson, actor

Skilled Mariners

Week 42

Franklin Roosevelt once said, "A smooth sea never made a skilled sailor." And, boy, are we learning to ride the waves.

On sunny days, when all goes as planned, it's pretty easy to take the time to breathe in, remember the values we want to live by, set our intentions, and be grateful for the moments. Yet life is made of all of it—the sunny days and the stormy ones.

And what we are seeing more than ever is the opportunity for each of us to step into the leadership of our lives. How do we want to show up for one another? What deeply matters? Are we willing and ready to take a moment to allow our energy to come back to our centers; move out of fear; allow ourselves to connect to our inner strength; and breathe up our internal ladder of energy into love, honesty, and creativity? No one can take away our inner power and choice of how we want to show up. We hold that courage within us.

It begins with a commitment to ourselves and the awareness of our shared connections. The storms will pass. As we allow the foundations of our being to grow deep and remember to see the wholeness of one another, our power to survive any storm strengthens.

I've long held Derek Mahon's poem "Everything Is Going to Be All Right" close to my heart. In these days of uncertainty, may we remember all that we are, remember our wholeness, gain the inner radiance that comes from reaching out to others with love and openness, and see one another. May we breathe in the powerful values of what matters most to each of us. These values are our unbreakable tools to navigate the roughest seas.

Sandy Schultz

Writing Prompts

1. What matters most to you?
2. How do you want to show up for them?
3. How will you reach out to someone to tell them?

"I Am" Statement

_____

_____

_____

"The breeze at dawn has secrets to tell you.
Don't go back to sleep."
— Rumi

Let Go and Gain Energy

Week 43

Last Sunday, on a sunny afternoon with a lazy, soft breeze, I was visiting some friends who had hammocks hanging in their yard. It's been a long time since I took a nap in a hammock, but it looked so tantalizing that I couldn't resist.

It took me a few minutes to get comfortable once I was in it. But eventually, as the sun flickered through the trees and the breeze gently rocked me, I felt my whole being give in to the experience. Muscles relaxed. I allowed myself to be held by a strong piece of cloth tied between two trees. I had so many ideas of what to write about this week, but the visceral feeling of trusting and fully letting go of tension was so powerful that it superseded them all.

How many things do we hold onto that tense our muscles (mentally, emotionally, and physically) and deplete our energy and our strength? How often do we allow ourselves just to be, to breathe, and to allow it to be easy? In physics, the term *zero point* refers to that moment of balance where no effort is needed to sustain momentum— or in the deepest cold, where everything becomes nothing, and nothing becomes everything. That's what I experienced lying in the hammock. Everything was okay. The world still turned without my doing anything.

Hours later, I still felt the power of allowing myself to be held by something else, something deeper, and it ignited huge energy and clarity for days following. That's what Six Minutes Daily is all about—being held by breathing in light, love, warmth, and joy and teaching our being to relax into that space and become a part of everything without effort. And then, from that touch of connection, possibility, and expansiveness, it's about allowing ourselves to clarify our intentions of how to walk into our days, giving gratitude, even if it's just for the ability to take our next breath. From this place of power, creativity rises and fear diminishes.

So, if you haven't relaxed, really relaxed, into a hammock lately, go find one and try it. Let yourself melt into all the magic and majesty that you are. Relax and breathe in the sunshine. And if you can't find a hammock, imagine one as you start your day with a few minutes of sitting quietly and breathing deeply. Then, write down an intention and something for which you are grateful. You'll be amazed by the power you can create.

Writing Prompts

1. What does it feel like to be held and supported?
2. What can you do to find that feeling more often?
3. How can you support someone else this week?

"I Am" Statement

_____

_____

_____

"Time will explain."
— Jane Austen

The Why of Time

Week 44

There is a lot of talk these days about time management with the insight that our most finite resource is not money but *time*. I teach about reflecting on the urgent versus the important, reviewing our hours, and putting them into various quadrants regarding productivity and thoughtfulness.

This week I decided to try something different. I tracked my time and wrote down what I did. And then, for each activity or behavior in that time, I asked myself, *Why? Why was I doing that activity? Why did I do it over and over?* And then I created another column next to the activities and asked myself the even deeper *why*.

It began to give me some really interesting realizations. It helped me see what rote muscle memory is. It helped me understand some of my deeper beliefs, unconscious patterns, and attitudes. And it began to show me places where my often-put-aside interests and curiosities continue to beckon, even if they seem far removed from my daily life.

And then crazy creativity and energy rose up inside of me. *What if* questions came up: *What if I gave a little more time to that calling, that why, and let go of some other things?*

It's a powerful thing when we allow ourselves to look at how we spend our time and ask ourselves why. It may lead nowhere or back to exactly where we are. Or it may illuminate a memory, ignite a little spark of an idea, or open a door to bring us back home to our authentic selves in powerful, loving, and wonderful ways. You never know until you try.

Writing Prompts

1. How do you spend your precious time in the morning?
2. Why?
3. Can you give yourself six minutes daily for self-care?

"I Am" Statement

_____

_____

_____

"We only live once, Snoopy."
"Wrong! We only die once. We live every day."
— Charles Schulz

Every Day

Week 45

This morning, a dear friend sent me a Charlie Brown cartoon with the above dialogue. Tickled by an inner kinship to Charles Schulz, I wanted to pass it on to you.

One of my big goals this year is to publish this book. In many ways, Snoopy's quote sums up why I'm writing a book. Leadership is all about how we choose to make the most of every day to lean into the values and vision by which we want to live. And that takes incredible courage, vulnerability, and personal responsibility.

Our ever-louder external world would love to define success for us. How many likes or retweets did we get? Which poll reinforces what we want to hear? What activities, accomplishments, or acquisitions came from the outer world to tell us we are worthy?

Somehow, it's never enough. But here's what we need to remember and internalize: *We are all so deeply, amazingly, powerfully worthy!* And we are learning. We fall sometimes and need to find the strength to get up again and again. That is the journey of life.

How do we learn not to get bruised every day? How do we find our own light and power when it seems pretty dark? How do we avoid falling into distraction, numbness, or depression just to pass the day when so much feels out of our control?

It starts quietly, with a few minutes of commitment to yourself. It starts by asking yourself three questions:

1. Who do I want to be today?
2. What values do I want to live by?

3. What is one super small thing I can do today to help embody that vision every day?

If you spend three minutes today breathing in that value or vision of the true you, two minutes writing down your intention around how you want to show up and what you want to embody for yourself today, and one minute writing down something for which you are grateful, you will have begun the practice of Six Minutes Daily.

See the miracle of life around you. Allow it in, no matter how small. We get to choose how we focus our attention.

I am not diminishing the powerful force of emotion. It's important to feel and to acknowledge our feelings. But let's also remember and make the internal commitment to ourselves that we are more than our feelings. We are the powerful mountain that still stands after the most ferocious of storms pass.

Writing prompts above

"I Am" Statement

_____

_____

_____

"Stop worrying about the potholes in the road
and enjoy the journey."
— Babs Hoffman, actress

Gratitude for the Road Less Traveled

Week 46

This morning, I awoke early to the joyful sound of a chorus of birds calling in the sunrise. Even now, several hours later as I write this, the birds continue to sing to the warm sun. It is a heart-expanding feeling, just to listen.

Following my youngest son's college graduation, I went on my own celebratory adventure walkabout in South America, where it was winter and only a few birds were singing. A group of like-minded travelers and I walked across salt deserts and sand deserts, up mountains, and through towns and ancient structures dating back hundreds and even thousands of years in Bolivia and Northern Chile. Clearly, we humans have been around a while. We looked up at night to see the Milky Way in its full glory and were wowed by the moon darkening the sun one afternoon during a full solar eclipse. We came to appreciate the days when we had indoor heat and hot water, and I am forever grateful for the warmth of alpaca blankets.

When I returned home to hug my beloved dogs, who are lying beside me now, my mind was filled with one word—*gratitude.* Gratitude for being born into the life I was; gratitude for the weather gods giving us sunshine; gratitude for the warm smiles of strangers when I bumble their language; gratitude for all the people who helped our adventure happen; gratitude for drivers who knew how to get deeply stuck four-by-fours out of ditches; gratitude for the joy that people with much less still embody; gratitude for so many everyday kindnesses; gratitude for my children's keeping our home in decent shape; and most of all, gratitude for the love I felt all around me.

Scott Peck opens his best-selling book *The Road Less Traveled* with a discussion about the idea that life is full of highs and lows and everything in between. He reminds us that if we acknowledge that kaleidoscope of experiences, then we can deeply appreciate the highs and understand the lows. He reminds us that we get to choose our mindsets throughout it all.

I first read his words over thirty years ago after people I deeply loved had died. I was in a very dark place. His words woke me up and helped bring me back.

That sense of appreciation and gratitude helps create a sense of ease and keeps tougher moments in perspective. I am even grateful for my five long hours of hugging the porcelain goddess after something I ate on our trip disagreed with me trip. Thank goodness my body could quickly get it out so I could go on with my adventure. I laughed and called it my unexpected digestive cleanse.

Perhaps some would call me Pollyannaish, but we only get so many days in this life. Why not be grateful for just the gift of life and breathe in the joy of all those birds still singing? Being grateful doesn't mean that we ignore injustice. It is about the balance of gratitude and standing up for our values. Gratitude heals us. It strengthens our leadership. And, well, gratitude just makes everything a little bit chirpier.

Writing Prompts

1. What are you grateful for this week?
2. What lessons have you learned through gratitude?
3. How can you be grateful for a challenge you are facing now?

"I Am" Statement

_____

_____

_____

"Life is everything. We can't escape that reality.
So let's learn to ride the rollercoaster."
— Unknown

The Magic of Forgiveness

Week 47

A few confessions: I have wondered about the meaning of life and why we're here for as long as I can remember. I also have always believed in magic. Growing up near a creek, I saw the magic in tadpoles' turning into frogs. I still feel magic in a darkroom as a white piece of paper awakens to an image after just a few seconds of light and some chemicals. And then there's the awareness that, one minute, you may not know someone, and the next, that person is forever a part of your soul.

Curiosity and wonder live in me every day. Rarely is there a day when I don't walk in the woods behind my house and give thanks for my feeling of being in Narnia.

I'm also so aware of the layers of life, responsibilities, and mistakes that can dampen that curiosity and darken wonder. Childhood optimism can seem naive when confronted with life's realities of betrayal, disillusionment, and loss. We all have our pain and our long lists of personal mistakes.

How can we believe that our internal container of joy also has the power to hold the most painful wounds, allowing us to stay open and creative versus closed in and tight, protecting our internal fortress?

One word—forgiveness. We need forgiveness of judging ourselves for not being perfect; forgiveness for judging others for not being what we wanted them to be; forgiveness while breathing in the knowledge that, no matter how bad or how hurtful, we were all doing the best we could at the time. Wow, that's hard. There are so many *but, but, buts* that spring to mind.

Yet it is the weight that comes of all that judgment that keeps us down, holds us back, and saps the energy of possibility. And we are the only ones who lose.

What if, instead of holding judgment, we forgave? And what if we asked ourselves, *How can we use our experience to grow and learn? What if we tried forgiving with the small steps?* For a few minutes, breathe in forgiveness and exhale anger. Let go of the victim. Allow the love. Notice what shifts. Write it down.

Viktor Frankl, in his book *Man's Search for Meaning*, shared his experience of noticing that some people in the most horrific times in Nazi concentration camps never lost their light. They forgave. They owned their internal power to choose how they showed up.

I believe that we can choose to never lose our light. It is still here, no matter how dim. And by practicing forgiveness, we can reclaim our power, wonder, and internal magic. And perhaps, just perhaps, that is why we are here.

Writing Prompts

1. Name someone with whom you are angry.
2. How does it feel to forgive them?
3. Can you forgive yourself?

"I Am" Statement

_____

_____

_____

"You doubt your value. Don't run from who you are."
— Aslan in *The Chronicles of Narnia:*
Prince Caspian by C. S. Lewis

Determination

Week 48

About twenty years ago, I began doing endurance races—long hikes, bike rides, marathons, triathlons, and so on. I'm no great athlete, and I completely buy into the concept that the tortoise wins the race. But something propelled me to race anyway. Perhaps I was hoping to keep in shape with three little boys running around or as a way to help my mental and emotional shadows fade.

In running, I learned that adrenaline kicks in during the first 20 percent of the event, and I power forward. And then in the great middle, fatigue comes, boredom enters, and energy leaves for 60 percent of the race. Those negative voices in my head become very loud. I can't go back, and the end is nowhere in sight.

I feel like that's where I am right now and where we are as a country, in the middle of a very long race with fatigue setting in. We are tired, and it is dark. And this is where true courage comes, from the power of our core. Determination propels me with a hyper focus on the steps in front of me.

If we take one step at a time, it's almost as if we can forget about the past or the future. The focus is just to keep going forward. There's no energy for anger or reflection or *what ifs*.

Those thoughts will do little to serve us in the amorphous middle of our current race. We need more self-care and more focus on the present to prevent us from stopping, giving in, or giving up. Deep inside, we must keep believing that light will come if only we can take one step in front of the other.

"When there is nothing left except the will which says to you hold on," Rudyard Kipling wrote.

When we do see the light in the distance, even if it's just a moment of laughter, energy comes and we can keep going for the last 20 percent. Out of nowhere, more energy comes. We find the strength and determination to make it.

Stories, myths, and legends have taught us that, if we are determined to keep going, our faith will be restored. I think of Shackleton and his crew of men who survived two years in Antarctica after their ship sank or the belief in the deeper, deeper magic of Aslan, the Lion, in C. S. Lewis's *Chronicles of Narnia*, as the embodiment of all that is good and just.

Yes, we may feel like we are in the great middle without much to hold onto. But now is the time to support one another, more than ever, to take another step forward. The light will come, along with real, visceral hugs.

Writing Prompts

1. What do you feel in the great middle of your greatest challenges?
2. How do you get through?
3. Can you think of a time when determination took you to a finish line?

"I Am" Statement

_____

_____

_____

Good Morning Pause

Week 49

Blessings for the Light
by David Whyte

I thank you, light, again,
for helping me to find
the outline of my daughter's face,
I thank you light,
for the subtle way
your merest touch gives shape
to such things I could
only learn to love
through your delicate instruction,
and I thank you, this morning
waking again,
most intimately and secretly
for your visible invisibility,
the way you make me look
at the face of the world
so that everything becomes
an eye to everything else
and so that strangely,
I also see myself being seen,
so that I can be born again
in that sight, so that
I can have this one other way
along with every other way,
to know that I am here.

Good morning. What if we chose every morning to really breathe in "good morning" for ourselves despite the sludge, the fears, the endless to-do list, and our concerns, from personal to global? How would it feel to decide to *own our mornings*, even for just a few minutes?

This is our gift. This is our choice. Someone said to me the other day, "It's dawning on me that from a bunch of different angles, you're asking us to slow down, check in, give our intentions and values a voice, say thank you, and bring our courageous souls to the world." I smiled. I teach what I must continue to deepen in my own learning. It's hard in our hyperactive culture.

But as more and more universities apply academic rigor to researching mindfulness, intention, and gratitude, the data continues to validate this message. It works. In improving leadership and organizations, it works. In improving health outcomes, it works. In improving self-worth and strengthening relationships, it works.

Check out Dr. Scott Snook's work at Harvard Business School. Look up the data from Larry Dossey and Joe Dispenza. Read the work of my teacher, Robert Holden.

Neurologist Richard Davidson from the University of Wisconsin says that he believes his grandchildren will think of mindful breathing and meditation in the same way we think of brushing our teeth today. *The data is compelling.*

So instead of just celebrating the big things this summer like graduations, weddings, birthdays, and holidays, try choosing to celebrate each day and take a few minutes to breathe in love every morning. Say good morning to the sun, the birds, your bed, the flowers, and your coffee, and give voice to your intentions and gratitude.

Writing Prompts

1. How do you say good morning to yourself?
2. What makes you smile in the morning?
3. How can you share that smile with someone you love?

"I Am" Statement

_____

_____

_____

> "You're never fully dressed without a smile."
> — *Annie*

What Makes You Smile Inside?

Week 50

We talk a lot about small steps, the little things that we do every day that can dramatically shift our mindsets, our trajectories, and our energy. Sometimes, though, it's hard, really hard—especially when we deal with loss or grief of any kind. So this week, I want to share some insights from other people who have deepened their intention setting with powerful shifts.

My closest childhood friend was laid off last year after a painful company restructuring. In the weeks that followed, she felt hurt, angry, and vulnerable. She told me that one of her inclinations was to change her computer password to some pretty angry words. Then she said that she heard a voice in her head saying, *How do I turn my anger into positive, powerful intentions?* So she changed one password to Fearless@56 and another to Empowered2020. Every time she opens her computer, she types "Fearless." That's a strong intention and reminder of how she wants to show up for herself.

Some incredible doors have opened to her in the last two months since her energy, drive, and awakened sense of self were activated. And the validating cycle keeps spinning upward.

If you find yourself saying, "Wow, that's hokey," so what? It works. When we find our smiles inside, it helps us bring better focus, clarity, and problem-solving creativity to our work and challenges.

Another friend lights a candle each morning, does his Six Minutes Daily, and finishes by playing some of his favorite songs from his childhood, like "Jukebox Hero" and "Gloria." Those beats and energy keep playing inside even when the day's events get tough.

My point is that we have the power to influence our energy and to shift our mindsets. Just think of what could happen if we gave ourselves more energy, more courage, more optimism, more patience, more listening, more space, and more thoughtfulness.

Yes, we need to walk through the fires and honesty of our feelings and emotions. We just don't need to get stuck there. We are so much more, so much deeper, so much more powerful than the emotions and events of the day that can fill our consciousness.

Writing Prompts

1. If you wanted to give yourself an inside smile, what would you change your password to?
2. What fun songs would you play to validate that feeling?
3. Are you smiling yet?

"I Am" Statement

_____

_____

_____

> "We're all in the mood for a melody,
> and you've got us feelin' all right."
> — "Piano Man," Billy Joel

Dimensions of Happiness

Week 51

Several years ago, I completed a weekend master coaching workshop with my mentor Steve Chandler. The workshop was held near Times Square, about as opposite to Jackson Hole, Wyoming, as one could get.

As we were leaving the seminar, someone mentioned that Billy Joel was playing at Madison Square Garden at 8:00 that night. The words barely registered with me until about seven thirty, when I had a surge of energy and decided to look online to see if there were tickets available. For eighty dollars, I could get second-level, center-stage seats. This blog could be entitled, "How to Go from Thinking about Going to Sleep to Running Down 7th Avenue to See Billy Joel in Fifteen Minutes or Less." But it's not. It's a blog about how to think about happiness.

As far back as Aristotle, people have talked about different levels of happiness. There's the *spontaneous, experiential, somewhat superficial level of happiness*—the surge we get from a new purchase, a fun dinner, Instagram likes, or going to a Billy Joel concert. It's the adrenaline rush, the fun story, the memory. Some writers call it the ego happiness—external things and experiences that just give us a cool zing. With social media leading the charge, this is often what we define as happiness, so we can end up zooming around trying to fill our cups with stuff, experiences, activities, and accolades, thinking this is full happiness. But it's really the thinnest of happiness.

Next, there's the *relationship level of happiness*. This is about the joy of connection, of love, of sharing the world with another, and of knowing that we aren't alone. This dimension of happiness brings in commitment and growth. Relationships aren't always easy or smooth sailing, but the synergy of 1 + 1 = 3 is real.

In the longest-running US study on human health and longevity (a large study run by Harvard since the 1930s), the only determinant of longevity the researchers can find is how connected we are in relationships. The more we are connected, the longer we live—and the higher levels of happiness we reach. At that Billy Joel concert, I sat next to a woman my age and her twenty-three-year-old daughter. She told me they had bought their tickets in February as birthday presents to each other. I was experiencing the concert at the level of a fun experience, while they were experiencing it at the level of deep joy, connection, and shared memories with each other. They laughed as they told me how they'd been singing his songs in the car since her daughter was a little girl.

Finally, there's the *purpose level of happiness*. This is the level where the deep work exists and where we make the daily commitment to uncover, ignite, and expand the values we want to live by, the gifts we want to share with the world, and the purpose for which we were born. This level of happiness has little to do with the first level, although it can sure have amazing, powerful, joyful, zinging moments. This is the container of happiness that includes frustration, exhaustion, practice, humility, resilience, and heart connection. That night, Billy Joel embodied this level of happiness. How many thousands of hours of practice has he put in over his lifetime to allow his fingers to now fly so effortlessly over the keyboard? His journey hasn't always been an easy one, but his joy as he played those ivory keys for the 111th time at MSG was palpable.

While we may not all have the musical gifts of Billy Joel, we do each have the power of harnessing our unique purpose within us. It is when we commit to courageously finding it, living by it, and learning to dance with the fears of our own insecurity, while we more joyously allow our gifts to be shared with the world, that the deepest happiness awaits us. It is the happiness of owning our lives, of creating our stories, and of breathing in our deepest knowing. A daily practice of setting aside our fears and quietly breathing can help that inner voice to be heard.

Then, when we show up in relationships, we bring more clarity, understanding, and honesty. Relationships can deepen, bringing more happiness.

When we commit to a daily practice of listening within, setting intentions, and allowing our beautiful selves to show up in the world, we open up to our most powerful happiness—the connection, acceptance, and love of ourselves.

Writing Prompts

1. What kind of experiences make you happy?
2. What relationship makes you happy?
3. What are you good at? Does it make you happy?

"I Am" Statement

_____

_____

_____

"Don't walk in front of me, I may not follow.
Don't walk behind me, I may not lead.
Just walk beside me and be my friend."
— Albert Camus

View from the Balcony

Week 52

Each Tuesday morning at 7:30 a.m., I have a forty-five-minute check-in with three lifelong friends where we discuss navigating the next chapter of life. We all met as we were just beginning our parenthood journeys. We all have similar professional backgrounds in consulting, business, and teaching, and we are now all creating our next chapters without the visceral chaos of children being front and center in our daily operations.

It's a complex transition, as are most transitions—full of excitement and possibility along with the full responsibility of deciding how we want to most powerfully use the 1,440 minutes we are given every day.

Decisions and choices around professional goals, relationship goals, health goals, and so on require an ongoing balancing act of clarity and prioritization. Our awareness that the dance of life is not eternal becomes more real. How do we define success? What do we want to accomplish, leave as our legacy, and love into each moment now?

A commonality we find is the vague but powerful fear that soon we will not be needed, which is crazy to define intellectually but very real in practice. As a result of this fear, it can be too easy to say yes to opportunities out of some shadow of uselessness before we think through how what's being asked of us fits into what we want. Having this trusted group of colleagues and friends listen, advise, support, and honestly critique our challenges in life is a game changer. It becomes a place of truth, accountability, and vulnerability. It's a powerful space to give voice to dreams, share, reflect, breathe, and receive trusted, real feedback.

Leading Our Lives from the Balcony

Harvard leadership professor Ron Heifitz says, "Leadership is about simultaneously playing the game and observing it as a whole.... It is about understanding how today's turns in the road will affect tomorrow's plan."

It's one thing to have goals and priorities and often quite another to put them in the calendar, read through the day, and see how it feels to meet all of the commitments you made to yourself and others. Which ones are the nonnegotiables we always get done, and which ones are the squishy commitments that often slide to the next day, week or month? And then, to ask ourselves the deeper questions of *why* and what we want to do about it further builds internal and external trust.

In addition to the daily practice of breathing, intention setting, and gratitude, creating and committing to a weekly accountability group of trusted friends or colleagues brings our dreams, fears, and hiccups out into the light, allowing us to view our lives from the balcony of broader vision along with checking in on our day-to-day progress of living life.

Try it. Find a couple of people you trust, and commit to thirty or forty-five minutes a week to share and listen. Set and share your goals for the year and milestones for the week within your different life roles. See where your commitments work and where they don't. Allow the growth that comes with opening up, sharing ideas and fears, and having the support to create new muscle memory. Here's to all the chapters that lie ahead.

Writing Prompts

1. Who are three or four people with whom you have mutual respect and trust?
2. What would it feel like to hold one another accountable?
3. Do you want to add them to your list of priorities?

"I Am" Statement

6

Quiet Shift; Seismic Change

Thanks for going on this journey toward attunement and deeper self-leadership. Remember, it is the ongoing practice that makes all the difference.

To keep up with weekly blogs, go to SixMinutesDaily.com and join. You can also download the SixMinutesDaily app on iPhone or Android to have an accountability support for your practice as well as keep your intentions and gratitudes in your confidential online journal.

Remember, it's in the *quiet shift* that we can create *seismic change* in how we feel, how we show up, and what paths unfold in front of us. The ripple effects, like throwing a stone in the water, expand far beyond what we may imagine.

References and Inspiring Books
I've Read on This Journey

1. *Dare to Lead* by Brené Brown
2. *Time Warrior* by Steve Chandler
3. *Seven Habits of Highly Effective People* by Stephen Covey
4. *The Emotional Life of Your Brain* by Richard Davidson with Sharon Begley
5. *Primal Leadership* by Daniel Goleman, Richard Boyatzis and Annie McKee
6. *Letting Go* by David R. Hawkins
7. *Power vs. Force* by David Hawkins
8. *Shift Happens!* by Robert Holden
9. *Loyalty to Your Soul* by Ron Hulnick
10. *Leadership in Turbulent Times* by Doris Kearns Goodwin
11. *Please Understand Me* by David Keirsey and Marilyn Bates
12. *Essentialism* by Greg McKeown
13. *The Inside-Out Revolution* by Michael Neill
14. *The Book of Awakening* by Mark Nepo
15. *Turning Pro* by Steven Pressfield
16. *Wisdom of the Enneagram* by Don Richard Riso and Russ Hudson
17. *Presence* by Peter Senge et al
18. *Leaders Eat Last* by Simon Sinek
19. *The Untethered Soul* by Michael Singer

About the Author

Sandy has spent her thirty-five-year career helping people and organizations develop their visions and make them thrive. Her passion is helping people find the bridge of inner energy, purpose, and alignment to create overall success and joy. Whether as a Procter & Gamble brand manager, assistant dean at Harvard University, cofounder of a successful marketing services company called Imagitas, or creator of the Start-Up Success Program in Wyoming, her passion is about helping people build thriving, abundant, healthy lives and organizations.

Sandy knows the joys and challenges of motherhood as a mom of three biological sons and two adopted children, along with providing a supportive home for many more. She also knows the pain of loss. Her earliest memory at age three is of being told her newborn sister had just died. Later, her father died when she was twenty-one. When her kids were teenagers, her husband one day thought he had a cold, but it turned out to be advanced brain cancer. Clearly, life is not something we can control, but we can learn to connect to our inner power to ride the waves, build broader awareness, and live thriving lives.

Sandy has her undergraduate degree from Northwestern University and master's degrees from Harvard University, Miami of Ohio, and the University of Santa Monica in the areas of public administration, organizational behavior, and spiritual psychology and consciousness. She is currently completing her PhD in depth psychology.

She is a lifelong adventurer and addicted snowboarder. She lives on a farm in Idaho with loved ones, including dogs, chickens, goats, and horses.